I DON'T SPEAK SPANISH

SPANISH

BUT I UNDERSTAND EVERYTHING WHEN I'M DANCING!

Rodney Eric López

I Don't Speak Spanish, But I Understand Everything When I'm Dancing!

ISBN Paperback: 979-8-89576-211-0
ISBN Hardback: 979-8-89576-212-7

Published by:

With every beat, shame softens. With every step, identity is reclaimed. This book is a reminder that belonging is not measured by fluency, but by heart—and that there are many beautiful ways to come home.

—Angélica Infante-Green,
former deputy commissioner of education, State of New York

Rodney speaks to a quiet but powerful reality many Latino families live every day, where language proficiency is too often treated as the gatekeeper to full acceptance within our own community. What this book makes clear is that Latino identity runs deeper than mastering Spanish, the language of our colonizers.

More than a memoir, this is an affirmation. Rodney's story is a necessary read for a new generation of Latinos to realize that identity is not something handed to you. Instead, it's something you have the right to claim and define for yourself.

With honesty and courage, Rodney names the tension of growing up Latino and hyphenated, navigating identity in rooms that demand a simplified version of who we are. He reminds us that choosing how we define ourselves, in every context, is an act of freedom and self-determination.

—Sami Haiman-Marrero,
CEO, URBANDER and author of *Becoming La Jefa*

Weaving childhood memories, family conversations, interviews with scholars, history, and social theory, López crafts a lyrical reclamation of Puerto Rican identity that insists on naming and claiming one's enoughness. This book holds grief, longing, and pain alongside resilience, hope, and choice—and in doing so, it expands our understanding of what authentic belonging can look like.

—**Jason Craige Harris**, strategist, writer, and thought leader

"I Don't Speak Spanish" is a beautiful and loving portrait of those Latinos who are pejoratively called "No Sabo" children and adults for their lack of comfort in speaking Spanish. In a memoir that elegantly weaves in important sociological and historical data, Lopez vividly illustrates how the policing of linguistic expression can be a racial project of erecting and reinforcing hierarchies. Yet, his story is a testament to how family and the joy of cultural expression can transcend those external limits on ethnic and racial identity. This is a much-needed intervention at just the right time.

—**Tanya Kateri Hernandez**,
author of *Racial Innocence: Unmasking Latino Anti-Black Bias and the Struggle for Equality.*

A powerful meditation on identity, rhythm, and return.

This book moved me deeply. It speaks to a quiet struggle so many carry — the shame of not speaking Spanish and the fear of not being "Latino enough." With honesty and vulnerability, the author names that ache and then transforms it.

What unfolds is not a story of deficiency, but of discovery. Through the rhythm of Salsa, he finds that language is more than words—it is memory, movement, ancestry, and pride. Culture lives in the body. It lives in the music. It lives in us.

DEDICATION

To Noni, my dance partner for life.
Te amo con todo mi corazón.

IN MEMORIAM

Willie Colón
1950 - 2026
A Bronx Nuyorican whose trombone changed Salsa and whose music
changed the world.

Ismael López, Jr.
1942 - 2024
"Cantando y acompañándose con música en su corazón."

TABLE OF CONTENTS

INTRODUCTION

I'm not into Harry Potter.

I've never read the books or seen any of the films. Not because I don't think it's a good story, I just haven't been inspired to make the time commitment. (Don't judge me.)

However, a friend of mine recently told me about an element of the story that intrigued me, so much so that I walked to my local library to pull one of the volumes off the shelf. It's featured in Chapter 30 of *Harry Potter and the Goblet of Fire*. Here, J.K. Rowling introduces The Pensieve: a stone basin in which swirls a silvery, misty-like substance. The magic bowl captures the young wizard's curiosity and draws him into its inner world. Once inside, Harry realizes that he is no longer in the "real" world but a witness to a series of memories from the mind of his mentor, Albus Dumbledore. He can see these memories in vivid detail but cannot interact with the characters inside them.

Upon returning to his reality, Harry learns that Dumbledore has so many memories that he can't keep them all in his mind. (Can you relate?) The Pensieve is a place for him to store his memories until he chooses to retrieve and analyze them later. Explaining the process to Harry, Dumbledore says:

"One simply siphons the excess thoughts from one's mind, pours them into the basin, and examines them at one's leisure. It becomes easier to spot patterns and links, you understand, when they are in this form."

While writing this book, there were so many times that I wished I had a Pensieve of my own. A magic place where I could step into my past, watch my memories come alive, and relive and record them with the distance of years and the perspective of the objective journalist. But that's not how memories work, right? Some are misty and fragmented, like what Harry saw before being sucked into the bowl. Others are as clear as the reflection in your mirror. I've learned that when writing about your life, you can use the tools that are available to you: photo albums, old videos, social media posts, interviews, and conversations with people who walked alongside you, and more. But at the end of the day, all you can do is be true to your recollection of events and share them as honestly as you can, knowing that memory is a fluid thing and that you don't remember things as *they* are, you remember them as *you* are.

While I strove to be as "factually accurate" as I could be in telling these stories, what endured in my life were not necessarily the facts. Rather, they were the emotions and the imprints they made, the decisions and actions they catalyzed, and the journey that I took as a professional, as an artist, as a dad, and as a human. Writing this book allowed me, like Dumbledore, "to spot patterns and links," without the magic wand.

And so what follows in these pages is my genuine attempt to tell the parts of my story that are in service of this book's themes: that your identity and culture are not solely defined by the language you speak, that the experiences of language acquisition and transmission are defined by more than just your personal choices, and that dance is a language of its own and one that is your birthright, whether you believe you have two left feet or not!

Why Now?

At the time of this writing, the United States is going through turbulent times, particularly for members of the Spanish-speaking community who are simply trying to earn a living and avail themselves of the opportunities that migrants and immigrants have enjoyed for generations. One of my relatives was recently honored at an award ceremony for Latino authors in California. A number of family members of several of the other awardees declined the opportunity to support their loved ones at the event due to the fear of arrest by government agents. This is just one example of the kind of anxiety Latino communities are feeling as both the discourse and government policy around citizenship and unauthorized immigration have become increasingly divisive and toxic.

As of March 2025, 30 states have adopted legislation establishing English as the official language within their jurisdictions. This kind of public policy can create difficult and even hostile conditions for non-English speakers in schools, hospitals, and other public forums. It's the kind of situation that has gained greater traction since academics like political scientist and former Harvard professor, Samuel Huntington, took rhetorical shots at immigrants from Latin America generally and Mexican-Americans, specifically.

"In this new era," wrote Huntington in his 2004 book, *Who Are We? The Challenges to America's National Identity*, "the single most immediate and most serious challenge to *America's traditional identity* [italics mine] comes from the immense and continuing immigration from Latin America, especially Mexico."

He continued, "'There is no Americano dream. There is only the American dream created by an Anglo-Protestant society. Mexican-Americans will share in that dream and in that society *only if they dream in English* [italics mine]."

Whether "English-only" messaging comes from the statehouse or the ivory tower, it's harmful. It belies the fact that most immigrants actually desire to learn English and become integrated members of their new nation, even if it isn't fast enough for Mr. Huntington.

While I'm a second-generation Puerto Rican born and raised in the great state of New York (the Boogie Down Bronx!), as you'll learn in the pages that follow, I can identify with those who are trying to make their way in a place where their native language is not welcome. I hope that, whether you speak English, Spanish, Spanglish, or any other heritage language, and feel any kind of inadequacy about it, the messages in this book resonate with you and serve as an invitation to put that burden down.

Note to the Reader

This book is more than just a recollection of personal stories. Through research and interviews, I've included the perspectives of experts in the fields of linguistics, bilingual education, dance, and race and ethnic studies. I'm grateful to all of the generous people who took the time to share their experiences and expertise with me. Some interviewees' names have been changed to protect their identities.

In the United States, Spanish-speaking people (or their non-Spanish-speaking relatives) are identified by many different names, which is one of the challenges I briefly address in this book. For decades, terms have been used that have been equally accepted and rejected by members of the community, including Latin, Spanish, Hispanic, Latino, Latinx, Latine, and more. While no name can accurately and completely capture a person's identity, for the purposes of this book, in addition to nationally specific identifiers, I will predominantly use Latino and

Latina. However, when quoting others, I will use the terms that appear in their texts.

One cannot do a thorough examination of the relationship between language and identity without including an analysis of race. While I do devote one chapter to how race, ethnicity, and language have intersected in my life, I recognize that there simply aren't enough pages to do this topic justice in a social memoir of this kind. I encourage you to read more of the work of the amazing experts featured in this book and explore these themes with your family and community.

Language shame is one of those things that we don't talk about much. It may just hang out in the background of our lives until we're put in a position that makes us feel "less than." Salsa was the way to a greater understanding of myself and my culture, in large part because it gave me a deep sense of joy and opportunity to play. It's my hope that whatever your relationship to language, there's something in this story that moves you.

Are you ready? Let's dance!

CHAPTER ONE

MIRA QUIÉN BAILA

The Univision reporter and I made small talk as my heart began to race in anticipation of the questions she would pose. Chatting before the interview was one thing, but would my Spanish be good enough for national TV? Prior to this moment, all of our preparation on the phone and in the minutes leading up to this interview had been conducted in English. Before I even had the chance to finish cobbling together a response to the first few questions, I stumbled, searching desperately for the words that were so practiced, polished, and professional for me in English but did not flow in my studied Spanish. Seeing how flustered I was, the reporter offered to let me answer in English and then have my words dubbed into Spanish during production. I nodded my assent dejectedly, feeling a deep, familiar shame.

You can clearly see the discomfort on my face when having to speak Spanish during this interview.

Univision, the premier Spanish-language media network in the U.S., requested an interview with me in the spring semester of 2013 when I was the National Program Director of Dancing Classrooms, an organization I found my way to through my role as a professional Salsa dancer and teacher. The interview was meant to support Univision's Education Week series, which highlighted education success stories across its programming. A student enrolled in one of our in-school residencies, a brilliant eighth grader named Karla Cariño, had been selected to be featured in one of these news segments. Within the organization, the energy around this opportunity was vibrant, and we were delighted at the chance to showcase the work we were doing, bringing social dance to schools.

Within the organization, I was the only Latino working at an executive level, and it naturally fell to me to promote our work and our students, liaising with Univision to include the context for Karla's participation in the TV spot. However, my Puerto Rican parents had decided not to speak Spanish to me while I was growing up in New York in the 1970s and '80s, and the stilted sentences I could put together were acquired later in life, starting with Spanish in high school. I kept finding myself in situations where it was assumed I spoke fluent Spanish. But my Spanish was far from fluent.

With my background in public relations and the strength of conviction I held for the program I was leading, I desperately wanted to perform well in the interview and be an asset to Dancing Classrooms. My nerves were already frayed as I prepared for the media appearance, worrying about how I would respond to off-the-cuff interview questions in a language I had struggled to acquire, despite my lifelong exposure to it. The truth is, I wasn't comfortable enough in Spanish to effectively represent my organization to the media, and that made me feel like a failure; or worse, an outsider, suspended between two places, a Caribbean archipelago where I would be seen as a foreigner and the United States where I would always be seen as different and other due to my ethnicity and race. *Ni de allí ni de acá.* [Neither from there, nor from here.]

When Univision first connected with the team at Dancing Classrooms, I was immediately attracted to the proposal. Knowing the role that Univision plays in Latino communities, I saw this as a coup for our organization and a special opportunity for our program and one of our students to be featured on Spanish-language TV. My position as National Director had pulled me a few degrees away from the day-to-day interface with students, so I worked with my colleagues to identify recommendations for students whose experience would align with their talents and aspirations. I was incredibly proud of our team when we recruited Karla.

As someone who was both born and raised in the Bronx and still lived there, I always welcomed the opportunity to work with a Bronx school. I was particularly proud when we had an opportunity to shine a positive spotlight on schools and children from the borough. I had once been a teaching artist at MS 498, The Van Nest Academy on Bronxdale Avenue. Walking into the school building, your eyes were drawn to huge, colorful banners highlighting the school's values, including one that was the hallmark of our program: Teamwork. High ceilings and huge windows that let in abundant sunlight make the lobby space welcoming and the perfect spot for a TV interview. Carol Ann Gilligan, the founding principal of this K-8 school, was a huge supporter of our program and always hospitable to us. She was instrumental in working with Karla and her mother to secure the necessary permissions to make this interview and appearance possible. Karla, a bright young woman who loved to dance and enjoyed every minute of the program we delivered in her school, showed her natural ability to adapt to new circumstances and connect creatively. Everything was falling into place.

Yet, my appearance on the newscast was dubbed, to my deep shame and visceral discomfort. When I was called on to represent Latinidad for my organization, I had fallen short. It was a huge win for Karla and for Dancing Classrooms. For me, it felt like a public embarrassment. I felt defeated, like I was not a real Puerto Rican. Still, I knew I could not face struggling through the questions with my basic, conversational Spanish and then suffer through the humiliation of having to speak English and be dubbed into the language my parents had spoken their entire lives, the language that has often been seen as an essential component of Puerto Rican and Latino identity.

While I was deep in my feelings, this was not the end for Karla.

Karla Cariño spoke beautifully about her experience with Dancing Classrooms.

A few months later, at the beginning of the fall semester for the 2013–2014 school year, Karla, now a high school freshman, was a member of our Weekend Academy program. Students who completed in-school residencies were eligible to continue their dance training with our faculty for up to five years. We were thrilled that Karla's enthusiasm for dance remained high and that she wanted to keep learning with us. That turned out to be fortuitous because Univision called back with an even bigger opportunity. On October 7th, they wanted to feature Karla as a special student dancer on the hit show, *Mira Quién Baila*, Univision's version of *Dancing with the Stars*. And once again, they asked if I would serve as the Dancing Classrooms representative on the show to talk about its wonderful, life-changing programs.

Not this time.

Ivelisse Garcia, appearing on the Univision TV spot. Ivelisse was a wonderful colleague whose fluency in Spanish helped positively represent our organization on the nationally televised *Mira Quién Baila*.

For the interview that would accompany Karla's appearance on *Mira Quién Baila*, I asked one of my colleagues, Ivelisse Garcia, born and raised in Puerto Rico, to do it in my place. Ivelisse was both a stellar teaching artist and an educational liaison for MS 498. Educational liaisons served as customer service managers for our arts residencies. In that role, Ivelisse was perfectly positioned to speak credibly about our relationship with the Van Nest Academy and the impact of our work on Karla and her classmates. Her ability to speak beautiful, conversational Spanish on camera starkly contrasted with my technically correct, but

noticeably uncomfortable Spanish, straight from a high school textbook.

Karla and her partner, Eddie Vega, executing a perfect cha-cha crossover break on *Mira Quién Baila!*

Karla's appearance on the show was a huge success. She and her Academy partner, Eddie Vega, danced a beautiful cha-cha with a confidence that belied her age and impressed the show's judges. Ivelisse shared important information about Dancing Classrooms across a television network in over 50 U.S. markets and many more in Latin America. I couldn't have been any happier for Karla[1] and her family and for the professionalism with which Ivelisse represented our work.

But was I salty and ashamed about my inability to speak Spanish? You bet.

Like many children of migrants, my inability to speak Spanish fluently was a growing source of disconnect, shame, and friction that I could no longer ignore.

---

[1] I recently caught up with Karla and learned that since her time with Dancing Classrooms, she went on to graduate from Lafayette College with a major in neuroscience and completed her master's degree in child development at Tufts University. She's now working with a university research team in California to develop an app that increases family engagement with their children in preschool classrooms and will be doing special outreach to the Latino community.

CHAPTER TWO

"SO HE WON'T UNDERSTAND"

"Borders, like diasporas, are not just places of imaginative intermingling and happy hybridities for us to celebrate. They are equally minefields, mobile territories of constant clashes with the Eurocenter's imposition of cultural fixity."
—Smadar Lavie and Ted Swedenburg

Origins

Despite my youth and the natural distortion of early childhood memories, I remember the words with a sharp clarity that can only be borne of something foundational. I was young, maybe five, in our family's house in the Bronx. My parents usually switched back and forth between English and Spanish when speaking to each other. However, they didn't speak Spanish to me directly, which meant I had extremely limited comprehension. Spanish was just a backdrop, like the Salsa music on the record player in the living room.

My parents were having an adult conversation, probably an argument, in English, when my mother turned to my father and said something so resounding in Spanish that I understood it. And I have never forgotten it.

Hable en español para que él no entienda.

"Speak in Spanish so he won't understand."

Everything surrounding this memory has become diffuse over time, but those words have never left me. Looking back from the vantage point of adulthood, now as a father and educator, I can take a generous view, seeing how my parents were code-switching to protect me from something they knew was not for my ears. But, for that little boy, hearing my mother so explicitly instruct my father to speak to her in a language I would not understand felt like a lever that flipped something inside me, one I spent decades trying to turn back again.

They could have asked me to leave the room or told me to go out and play, but instead, they chose to use the language barrier between the first and second generations in our household as a shield. There was deep pain in realizing, even as a young child, that significant meaning was beyond my grasp because I lacked the language of my parents, my family, my community, and the proud history that is our foundation.

My very first trip to Puerto Rico at three years old included a ride on this tricycle. My earliest years were immersed in Spanish, but I would always understand more than I could ever speak.

The Great Migration

Dad and Mom at a party in the early 70s. They came from neighboring towns in Puerto Rico and spoke Spanish to each other but chose to speak with me in English.

My parents both arrived in New York from Puerto Rico on the tail end of what is now known as the Great Migration. As the archipelago moved away from an agrarian, sugarcane-centered economy toward industrialization in the decades after WWII, many Puerto Ricans joined the burgeoning diaspora and migrated to cities like New York in the United States. "Hundreds of thousands of people migrated without knowing that they were being socially and collectively ejected as part of a calculated government move," Jorell Meléndez-Badillo explains in his book *Puerto Rico: A National History*. Among those hundreds of thousands, seen by the government of the day as a necessary expulsion, reducing the population to allow for industrialization and prosperity that was never fully realized on the archipelago, were my grandfather, my dad, and eventually, my mom.

Migration has always been part of the DNA of the people who make *Borikén*, the Taíno name for Puerto Rico and origin of our affectionate denominator, *Boricua*, their home.[2] According to Meléndez-Badillo, the archipelago, strung between the Island of Hispaniola (Haiti and the Dominican Republic) and the Virgin Islands, due north of the coast of Venezuela, has been inhabited by peoples who are defined by travel, migration, and open engagement with new peoples and ideas.

Yet, the meeting of peoples was not always peaceful, and early contact with Spanish explorers quickly became a devastating new reality for the Taíno. Spanish colonizers, as they perpetrated a vicious conquest of the local Indigenous people, sought a new source of racialized and oppressed labor, bringing the first enslaved Africans to the archipelago in 1517. It was only a decade later when enslaved people staged the first slave revolt in Puerto Rico, the beginning of a long, ongoing struggle for freedom from enslavement and racism.

From these origins arose the triple identity that Puerto Rican institutions would later embrace: Puerto Ricans are the descendants of the Taíno, free and enslaved Africans, and the Spanish. "The Great Puerto Rican Family," a topic I will explore further, is shown by Meléndez-Badillo to be not only a foundational myth, a reclamation of our identity beyond the exaltation of the Spanish, but a dangerous tool in the hands of later regimes that twisted it to delegitimize our African

---

[2] "With the decline of the Taínos, their Arawak language was lost. A few Arawak borrowings into Spanish (and English via Spanish) have endured, including *huracán, tabaco,* and *guayaba* ('hurricane, tobacco, guava'). And many Puerto Ricans of all ethnoracial backgrounds refer to the island as *Boriquén* or *Borínquen,* and to themselves as *Boricuas,* all of which derive from Arawak terms." *Puerto Rico: A National History,* by Jorell Meléndez-Badillo

and Indigenous origins, at times reducing African roots to folklore and promoting the extinction myth about the Taíno.

Great PR Family: Artistic representation of the Great Puerto Rican Family concept by pyrographer Wilfredo Santiago.

In the last half of the 19th century, a precarious situation emerged as Puerto Ricans sought independence from Spain. Taking advantage of a weakened Spanish colonial power, the United States saw an opportunity to expand its presence in the Caribbean, establish a military base, and advance its aim of building a canal across the isthmus of Panama. As a result of this conflict and the broader Spanish-American War, Spain formally ceded Puerto Rico to the United States in 1898. The question of Puerto Rico's status in relation to the United States (unincorporated territory, statehood, or independence) has shifted over the decades, remaining a highly contested issue into the present.

After earlier waves of migration to the United States in the 1930s and earlier, Puerto Ricans began to migrate north en masse, with around

835,000 leaving the archipelago between the 1940s and 1970s, driven out by industrialization and a political project aimed at reducing the island nation's population, according to Meléndez-Badillo.

Caribbean culture, as scholars such as Antonío Benítez-Rojo and Juliet McMains argue in her book *Spinning Mambo Into Salsa: Caribbean Dance in Global Commerce*, is defined by "supersyncretism." This propensity to combine elements of cultures and traditions, creating new art forms, ways of being, and expressive cultural products through contact between distinct groups, was on full display during the Great Migration and my parents' arrivals in New York. From the famous Palladium to smaller clubs like the ones my dad played in as a Salsa musician, music became the ultimate expression of this explosion of defiantly joyful cultural creation. Joshua Jelly-Schapiro describes this process in his book *Island People: The Caribbean and the World*, saying:

> "The city's metro region is today home to more than a million people who identify with Puerto Rico by birth or heritage. The presence of these 'Nuyoricans' in the United States, and the lives they've made there, have had a profound impact not only on New York but on their home island—a place whose culture has long been shaped at least as much by those who have left the island as by those who have stayed. In the 1960s and after, emigrants' kids reimagined Afro-Cuban music on their parents' congas to make 'Salsa' become the sonic lingua franca of 'Latin New York.'"

As hundreds and thousands of people arrived from the warm, year-round tropical climate of Puerto Rico to the cold winters of New York, we were adding valuable cultural production to the United States beyond the roles we had been relegated to as a class of workers, our contributions helping to build a greater racial democracy in the place we came to call home.

Arriving in New York: My Mom

A terrible family tragedy precipitated my mother's journey from her home in Guayama at just eighteen years old. As the fifth of eleven children, she faced many of the same challenges as other working-class Puerto Ricans in the early 1970s.

An 11-year-old Rodney with my mom and cousin Ivia on a Christmas visit to my mom's hometown in Puerto Rico. When she arrived in New York, she became very self-conscious about her ability to speak English.

Although she told me in a recent conversation that she has fond memories of climbing trees and playing marbles as a girl, she also dealt with the burden of helping raise her younger siblings. Despite her love of learning and school, she had to leave high school before she could graduate. She was needed at home as a caregiver.

My mother received English instruction at school only after the sixth grade, but the primary language of instruction throughout her school years was Spanish. She explained to me that the biggest challenge she had to overcome after moving to New York was unlearning things she had picked up in school that reflected the level of English instruction in Puerto Rico. She had learned to speak English with an unfiltered Spanish accent and was surprised to realize that English speakers often did not understand her. However, her biggest critics were other Spanish speakers who had already progressed further with their English fluency.

Pineapples

Telling me about her early experiences trying to speak English in New York, Mom recounted going to a local supermarket to buy fruit. As usual, in those early days, she scanned for Mexicans or other people working in the supermarket who looked like they might be able to communicate with her in Spanish. Finally, she gathered up her courage to try to buy a pineapple in English.

Holding the fruit, so different from the fresh, local fruit she must have eaten in Puerto Rico, my mom could not figure out if it was ripe. She would have to ask.

"Is it rape?" She asked a stockist.

"Rape?"

The stockist was appalled, not understanding what Mom was trying to communicate. Was the pineapple rape? What was this woman talking about?

My mother, upon realizing her error, was mortified. The memory has stuck with her for all these years, a pivotal moment of shame, but also the grit that drove her to not give up and instead redouble her efforts to improve her accent and vocabulary so that she would never again say "rape" instead of "ripe."

Arriving in New York: My Dad

A teenage Ismael López Jr., like hundreds of thousands of Puerto Ricans, came to New York in search of better economic opportunities.

My dad had already established himself in New York years prior, seeking opportunities for work and an escape from poverty. He had prior relationships before meeting my mom, from which came my lively older half-siblings. Arriving with very little English or formal education, it was through work and his involvement in the union movement that he strengthened his ties to the U.S. and became confident in his ability to speak English. In fact, Dad was the first Puerto Rican union president in New York, something he was rightfully proud of. For him, involvement in union politics was a turning point as he was mentored, supported, and encouraged not to let his level of English hold him back. In shedding his shame about his accent and putting himself out there, he gained the opportunities he needed to grow as a professional and a bilingual Puerto Rican in New York.

He also had deep roots in the community, working for many years on the side as a percussionist in Salsa bands and in a number of side hustles. During my childhood, I never imagined the role that this music and years of listening to the radio with Mom would play in my career and my ability to eventually reclaim my Puerto Rican identity.

In addition to working several jobs after moving from Puerto Rico, Dad also played congas in local Salsa bands in New York.

Failing the Test

Before his passing in 2024, I conducted a series of interviews with my father, exploring his life and the experiences that made him the man he became. Dad told me about working in a garment factory when he arrived in New York, earning less than a dollar an hour. He learned how to sew and spent hours bent over the machines, trying to move quickly, and feeling exploited. With a growing family to provide for, my dad knew there had to be something better out there. A friend of his from a Salsa band got a job at Manhattan State Hospital in maintenance, and he convinced my dad to apply there as well.

When my dad dialed the number his friend gave him as a contact at the hospital, he reached the hospital director, immediately feeling out of his depth. "What the hell did I know about how to talk to a director?" he said of the experience. The receptionist who greeted him when he went for an in-person follow-up, a Puerto Rican woman, looked at him like, "This guy is a *jíbaro*, what is [he] going to see the director for? [He] couldn't even speak English!"[3]

The director wrote a note for my dad and sent him back to the receptionist, who looked at him like, "This guy is well connected," now that he had a note from the director in hand. But my dad told me that, at this point, he was still barely able to understand what was happening. He was sent to classes intended to teach the incoming maintenance workers how to do the job. My dad, knowing his English would not be up to the task, sat at the back of the class and just hoped the instructor wouldn't call on him. When it was time to take the test, my dad failed the first, second, and third tests. Everyone passed, except my dad. He told himself he didn't want that job, that he couldn't do it anyway.

The instructor called my dad to speak with her as the other participants walked out of the room, diplomas in hand. As my dad sat before this instructor, she said, "Mr. Lopez, you didn't make it." At that, my father started crying, and the instructor joined him. He got up to go, and this empathetic woman, deeply moved by how hard my dad was struggling, not knowing the language, asked him to wait for a moment, come back into the room, and told him, "You passed!"

That job became the opportunity that helped my dad provide for his family for years and eventually launched him into union politics. With

---

[3] A Puerto Rican small farmer, rural worker, or laborer, especially of mountainous regions, per Merriam-Webster.

more exposure to English and reason to learn the language, he gained confidence and pride in his bilingualism.

Why Couldn't I Understand Spanish?

If Spanish was so tied to Puerto Rican pride and wrapped up in the creative, cultural movements that arose in the diaspora, why didn't my parents teach it to me? I know my parents would have liked me to learn Spanish, but their focus was elsewhere. During my early years, my mom continued to work on her English, which was harder to do as a homemaker with few English speakers to practice with. I sometimes wonder if she spoke English to me, in part, because she needed a conversation partner. My dad was a busy breadwinner, and our family lacked the community resources we would have needed to be successful in maintaining the minority language into the next generation. For years, I felt resentment, shame, and grief as I wondered why my mom and dad had not taken advantage of my early years to pass their language on to me, and I saw Spanish as the only key to addressing the deficit at the root of my identity and ability to feel whole as a Puerto Rican.

Tempering the pain, even resentment, and loss I felt because of my lack of Spanish in childhood, and the resulting cultural disconnect, led me to a growing realization that there was something much bigger than individual choices at work.

All the Siblings, Lined Up in Order of Fluency

While writing this book, I came across an article in *The New York Times* that grabbed my attention. "The Guilt of Not Being Bilingual" was written by George Gene Gustines, and I felt deeply aligned with what I was reading. George shared that his parents moved from Ecuador to New York, and he never developed fluency in Spanish. I reached out and was honored to meet George to talk at length about his experience.

In the article, George shares a line that stuck with me: "If you lined up my siblings from eldest to youngest (me), you would hear the diminishing fluency in Spanish." This line speaks directly to the fact that our fluency, or lack of it, is not a function of our own aptitude, intelligence, or respect for our heritage culture. It is largely shaped by our circumstances, as we see in George's family, where each child had less exposure to and less support and positive reinforcement for Spanish, as the pressures of assimilation in the U.S. were exerted over larger portions of their lives.

After a childhood of passive bilingualism, in which George understood what people said to him but avoided responding in Spanish, instead using English, he now laments what he considers a "deficiency":

"I always tell people that for me, Spanish lives in this in-between place. I understand almost everything as long as it's not coming at me too fast, but speaking is another story. I hesitate, I overthink every word, and because I so rarely use the language out loud, the hesitation just gets worse. On the occasions when I have to speak it, I feel like I sound terrible, and that makes me want to avoid speaking it even more. It becomes this cycle where the less I use it, the less confident I feel, and the less confident I feel, the less I want to open my mouth at all."

I was grateful to process some of these dynamics with Dr. Elaine Ruiz-López, an accomplished educator, a champion of bilingual education in New York City, CEO of the International Leadership Charter School (the first charter high school in the Bronx), a bestselling author, and, oh, my sister-in-law. My interview with Elaine illuminated a key element of the language loss in my family. Political and social agendas, sometimes stated and sometimes based on deep cultural assumptions about newcomers and language, stood firmly in our way, making Spanish acquisition in my childhood a losing battle. The situation was manufactured for me long before my birth, and the lack of resources to support bilingualism in a second-generation Puerto Rican kid was by design, not a simple omission.

Tearing Down *That* Myth About Bilingualism

A persistent myth says that bilingual children become confused and their literacy and fluency in the dominant language is hindered by speaking a minority language, either as their native language or a co-native language. Many parents, like mine, internalized this, leading them to focus primarily on English. Spanish was only a nice-to-have, but English was a non-negotiable, so they focused on English during our childhoods, missing out on the opportunity to sufficiently expose us to Spanish. What parent wants their child to struggle, as they themselves did, to navigate a world in which their accent and language status serves as a formidable barrier? Who wants to work hard to overcome this challenge only to realize that greater fluency in English can never fully erase the mark of being "other"?

Elaine explained to me that dozens of researchers in the 1970s, including groundbreaking work by Dr. Jim Cummins at the University of Toronto, have shown that the myth about language confusion does not play out in the real world. His research proposed key theories, such as Common Underlying Proficiency and the Linguistic Interdependence Hypothesis, advocating the use of students' home languages as assets. It challenges assimilationist educational models to promote critical literacy and empower multilingual learners. His research refuted the notion that switching languages between home and school harms learning, showing instead that strong first-language skills support development in a second language.

The fears about fluency and academic success in English when a minority language is spoken at home are just that: fears. In fact, as Elaine described, the native language of a child's family must be acknowledged not only in its cultural context but also because of the cognitive function of a student, a child who's living in two worlds.

Elaine went on to elaborate on this important point further:

> "That is a myth. It is not rooted in fact or in research. Children, as well as adolescents, are not necessarily confused because of the language of instruction. It has to do with methodology, with the quality of instruction, and with what the literature on teaching pedagogy describes as differentiation and scaffolding of instruction. A child who is a non-native speaker of English goes into a classroom, and there is a process that is part of second language acquisition. As a child, I was that student: going into the classroom, listening, observing, and processing. There is a very intentional pedagogy and methodology in bilingual instruction— one that I did not have."

Without institutional acknowledgement of the presence of Spanish in New York in the 1970s and 1980s, facing deeply entrenched negative views about bilingualism, and trying to shield me from the xenophobia they had experienced, my parents chose English for me well before I stepped foot into school for the first time.

Where Do We Fit In?

Born in 1974, I came into the world alongside the Salsa movement, and, just like Salsa, I have had to make careful sense of an identity Americans seemed unable to name or see as a whole, vibrant, multifaceted self. Regardless of what nativist Americans may have thought about it, by the time I was born in New York, Caribbeans had arrived, and we were building communities that reflected the culture and language we brought with us. The Great Migration gave rise to cultural syncretism, a thriving community of *Boricuas* in New York and other cities in the U.S. (now numbering 6.1 million Puerto Ricans living stateside, according to 2024 Census Bureau data published by the Pew Research Center), and the constant push-pull between cultural adaptation and the pressure to assimilate. Even as our parents and grandparents were expected to keep their heads down, work menial labor, and assimilate into the dominant culture, they resisted with joyful artistic and cultural expressions and a wholehearted embrace of syncretism, blending elements to build something beautiful.

CHAPTER THREE

NEVER ENOUGH

Que siempre fue la lengua compañera del imperio.
"Language has always been the companion of empire."
—*Gramática Castellana*, Antonio de Nebrija, 1492

"Language ideologies are belief systems about language and the people who speak in a particular way. Such beliefs are never about language alone. Ideologies about language are also tied to ideologies about social identity, nationalism, and other important processes."
—*Immigrant Spanish as Liability or Asset? Generational Diversity in Language Ideologies at School*, by Allard et al.

As second and third-generation children of migrants and immigrants, we are left to pick up the distributed and scattered pieces of our identity. My relationship to the Spanish language has always been complicated. Speaking Spanish, or not speaking it, has marked my Puerto Rican identity in ways I am still unraveling. For most of my life, I've wrestled with how to claim my own identity without speaking the language that is a marker for it and a currency for connection in my community. Throughout my childhood and well into adulthood, the realization that my parents' language was just beyond my grasp was a source of shame. For me, Spanish was not a part of childhood; it arrived later, in high school.

But by the time you are learning Spanish in high school, it doesn't sound like the language of your family. It doesn't sound like the voices on the block. Instead, it carries the awkwardness of a textbook, the stiffness of conjugation drills, and vocabulary lists. And people notice. People have things to say about Spanish that sounds like it came from a classroom instead of a home. I began to feel my body tensing up even at the thought of speaking Spanish, and my shame did not dissipate as I learned the basics; instead, I was faced with more opportunities to fail and fall short as a Puerto Rican, leaving me adrift between an American identity I could not fully claim and a Puerto Rican one I believed would not claim me.

Paola Ramos describes this strange purgatory well in her book, *Defectors: The Rise of the Latino Right and What It Means for America*. She explains that:

> "As opposed to many white Americans, Latinos have to work twice as hard to not just feel 'American' but to be accepted as 'American' by the larger society. Assimilation is a contractual agreement; it can only work if both parties agree to the terms."

Meanwhile, as Elaine Allard described in her research, Spanish is seen as intrinsically linked to Latino identities. For me, and possibly for you as well, the internalized need to prove ourselves as Americans, or face the social consequences for failure to do so, and a strange sense that Spanish should just come naturally to us, be in our blood, became the root of an identity based on deficit.

The "No Sabo" Kids

I am watching an older news clip, which at this point may be even a decade old, from the aftermath of a *Copa América* match Mexico won in the United States. A smooth-talking reporter with a polished accent stands in front of a large crowd of revelers, looking for someone to interview about this jubilant moment. I see a young child with a fresh haircut and large brown eyes come onto the screen as the reporter pulls him in front of the camera and the scene unfolds.

The reporter asks, breathlessly, in his rapid-fire Spanish:

Hijo de México. Nene, veni, veni, veni. ¿Cómo te llamas?

"Son of Mexico. Come here, kiddo, come on, come on, what's your name?"

The child looks bewildered. I can feel my own body tensing as I watch him, realizing that he has been ambushed, thrown onto live TV in a language he doesn't speak.

"My, my, my name?" the child stutters out, even as the reporter continues the barrage of questions, not waiting for the child to catch up.

¿Por qué gana México? ¿Por el Chaquito Giménez, el técnico? ¿Cómo te sientes?

"Why did Mexico win? Because of Chaquito Giménez, the coach? How are you feeling?"

Confusion. Panic. Shame. I feel it all wash through me, making my stomach drop, as I watch the kid clearly wishing desperately that he was anywhere but there, anywhere but the place where he had been, until moments before, swept up in the celebratory moment with the rest of Team Mexico's fans. I can feel this in my own body as I watch him, overcome with a sensation that goes well beyond empathy. This is something deeper, something I, too, have felt and still carry with me.

Child: "What?"

Reporter: *No, no, está muy emocionado.*

"No, no, he's too excited."

The reporter tries to brush off the child's clear, desperate, resounding lack of comprehension. A voice from beyond the camera, baritone yet clear, says:

No entiende.

"He doesn't understand."

This clip is an early example of what has now become standard fodder for social media virality: videos of kids people think *should* be able to speak and understand Spanish failing at the task. In fact, one tweet that went viral after this exchange aired on TV, written in all caps, read: "RAISE YOUR KIDS NOT TO BE 'YO NO SABO.'"

Spanish is a very regular language compared to other romance languages like Portuguese or French, meaning the verbs mostly follow a set pattern of conjugation. However, many of the most used verbs, in particular "to be" and "to know," do not follow the pattern. Children, even native Spanish speakers in Spanish-majority contexts, sometimes make the mistake of bending these irregular verbs to the pattern they think should apply. So *sé*, the irregular conjugation of *saber* ("to know") in the first person, present tense, becomes *sabo*, mimicking the usual pattern of first-person, present-tense verbs that end with "-o."

The term *no sabo* is a more recent expression, but seeing countless videos gain viral notoriety as they spark debates among the Latino community and the countries we hold ties to, I never stopped feeling sick with the knowledge that I was perceived in the same way, just blessedly not blasted across the social media platforms as a disgrace to my own identity.

But what if *no sabo* kids are becoming the norm? According to Mark Hugo López, director of race and ethnicity research at the Pew Research Center, 85% of Latinos say it is important for future generations of Latinos in the U.S. to speak Spanish. This is the same demographic responding to videos of kids like the boy who couldn't understand a reporter after a match, with concern for the future of Latinos in the U.S. Even in the third generation, the majority of Latino parents still want their kids to speak Spanish and try to pass it on.

Despite these intentions, younger people and third-generation Latinos are the least likely to be Spanish speakers, which is significant because the third generation is the fastest-growing group in the Latino population. Immigration has increased in recent years, but the cake is already baked, meaning the shift toward English is already well underway. A generation of young Latinos is coming of age in an English-only environment. They play games in English, watch television in English, go to English-language movies, and listen to music in English.

Mark described this almost performative aspect of the idea that Spanish is on the rise in the following way:

> "Every now and then, there are stories about Spanish being on the rise because Latinos are reshaping America. One or two songs by an artist from Latin America might become number one in the U.S. or even around the world. That's great, but the problem is that it hasn't been sustained. Oftentimes these moments are one-time shots, and they don't last."

We can see from this research that it isn't just my family or yours that has a complicated relationship with Spanish. The complicated, nuanced set of feelings many of us hold about the language combines aspiration and language for connection with frustration and even shame. So when

I think about Spanish and the Latino population, it feels complicated. Yet the reality is, most young Latinos are growing up in environments where English dominates, and Spanish fluency is becoming less common.

And into this mixture of longing and shame come reporters like the one who interrogated a boy who clearly did not understand what he was saying. Into that delicate realm between losing one language and gaining another step the hundreds and thousands of people commenting on those videos, mocking the *no sabo* kids.

In 2023, López and the Pew Research Center's research uncovered a staggering, if not surprising, figure: the majority of Latino participants had been mocked, made fun of, and humiliated, or had seen firsthand as someone else was mocked and embarrassed, for not speaking Spanish.

Not Enough Spanish

We had a church hymnal in our house, a gift from an earlier time when going to church was a more regular part of my mother's life. The praise book was in Spanish, and I remember my dad reading it to me as a young child in that sing-song voice adults use when teaching kids words. The cover was leather-bound in a rich maroon, and I can still see his strong brown fingers, shaped by a lifetime of hard work, turning the pages and underscoring the words as he slowly went through the scripture with me, showing me how to pronounce each one.

Cantando y acompañándose con música en su corazón.

"Singing and accompanying yourselves with music in your hearts."

My father was a formally uneducated man, yet his intelligence enabled him to accomplish a great deal in life, despite the cards he was dealt. He was a reader and valued language in general. I felt, in those precious moments, with the maroon book in our hands, a deep longing I did not have words to describe. It was clear, even as a small boy, that my dad's small efforts would not be enough for me to become fluent in Spanish, but I soaked up the moments of connection.

Having my parents enact small gestures—speaking to me in Spanish as a baby, reading from the hymn book to me, my dad teaching me tongue twisters as a teenager—and even enrolling in Spanish classes in high school was never going to be enough to provide the exposure and education I needed for fluency, leaving me with an identity deficit and a desire to feel like I belonged.

Never Enough

As I shared my story and spoke with others who had similar experiences, a framework described by Pilar Garces-Conejos Blitvich in her article "You are shamed for speaking it or for not speaking it good enough: The paradoxical status of Spanish in the US Latino community" helped explain the different ways this has shown up in our lives.

Garces identifies five ways people relate to Spanish when they do not speak it fluently. I have found these categories useful in conversations with dozens of people about their experiences, and I recognize that I have felt more than one of these at different times in my own life. They can be seen as a spectrum, often overlapping or appearing in combination. The first, "Enoughness," describes people who feel they know enough Spanish to be considered authentically Latino. The second, "Neoliberal Views," refers to those who emphasize personal responsibility, believing it is up to them, rather than to external systems, to preserve or pass on the language. The third, "Emotion," captures the strong feelings, including frustration, guilt, and longing, that arise around not being fluent. The fourth, "Critical Views," sees structural barriers, such as institutions or societal pressure, as the main obstacles to learning or using Spanish. Finally, "Essentialism" reflects the belief that language is deeply tied to cultural or personal identity.

For some of the people I spoke to, there was a solid sense of identity. Elaine described how she always identified as *Boricua* or Puerto Rican, going toe-to-toe with anyone who challenged her or called her *Americana*. For her, the Jones Act of 1917, granting Puerto Ricans U.S. citizenship, meant that it was enough to say she was Puerto Rican; the American part could be implied rather than hyphenated.

Split between New York and Florida, it's rare for all my siblings to be together, but here we are at a recent family reunion. L–R: Robert, Leslie, Yvonne, Dennis, Tony, Lisa, me, and Janet (seated).

But there is a stark difference between Elaine's experience and my own, or that of my siblings, who all related feeling disconnected and lost in a strange limbo between Latino, Black, and American at different times in their lives. The difference is that Elaine grew up speaking fluent

Spanish. When she visited the archipelago as a child and was called a *gringa*, she could hit back, having been "mothered in the native language."

Eight Is Enough

My eldest sister, Janet, described being ridiculed for her broken Spanish by cousins and extended family in the Bronx, and our sister, Yvonne, had similar memories, adding that she felt limited to standard greetings like *bendición* (blessings) to show respect for older family members. Everyone had stories about being laughed at and shutting down to some extent, overcome by shame. Yvonne summed it up by saying, "I felt like an American speaking Spanish."

Anthony, my older brother, described relatives ridiculing him and feeling as though he had to prepare in advance what he was going to say to get it right. Growing up, Leslie wanted a connection with her maternal grandmother but couldn't speak to her due to the language barrier.

Lisa, working at Walmart, realized she had some catching up to do to help customers who did not speak English well. She got to work learning, and a budding "addiction" to *telenovelas* (soap operas) soon helped her immerse herself at home and at work, finally making the progress she wanted with the language of our forefathers and foremothers.

Somehow, in different ways, my siblings and I all experienced feeling we were not enough: not Puerto Rican enough, not Latino enough, not really Black, and never American enough. Each of us took different approaches and had different experiences, but we all related to a sense of loss and grief, realizing that our lack of fluency in Spanish as children made us outsiders in our own selves.

During a powerful conversation with George Gustines, *The New York Times* writer whose parents immigrated from Ecuador to New York, he shared a difficult story about studying Spanish in high school.

"I hated public speaking to begin with, and having to give an oral report in Spanish made everything worse. My pronunciation felt terrible, and I was so nervous that my teacher joked I looked like Little Orphan Annie because he could only see the whites of my eyes with my head down the whole time."

Mark Hugo López is the director of race and ethnicity research at the Pew Research Center. His life experience and professional insights on language and identity are informative.

I had the pleasure of interviewing Mark Hugo López, director of race and ethnicity research at the Pew Research Center. Mark, a third-generation Mexican-American whose grandparents immigrated to the Los Angeles area during the Mexican Civil War as children, recalled his parents' Chicano pride and commitment to passing this on to their children.[4] Despite this pride, Mark's parents' efforts to pass fluent Spanish down to their third-generation kids were not enough to offset the pressures of English dominance. Every Saturday, Mark's parents insisted that the whole family speak only Spanish—"Spanish Saturdays," they called it— but, as in my family, these gestures were not enough to counter the dominance of English and foster bilingualism. Mark was questioned

---

[4] Often referred to as the Mexican Revolution, this armed conflict took place between 1910 and 1920.

about where his lack of fluency fit in with his strong Chicano identity while attending university and told me about an interaction early in his own teaching career when a white professor spoke broken Spanish to him and was deeply disappointed when Mark asked to switch to English. Adding to this, Mark was often made to feel like an imposter because of his fair complexion. Being relentlessly asked to prove his connection to his own community left Mark with a chip on his shoulder.

But that's not the end of Mark's story with language. When he applied to work at the Pew Research Center, part of the job was the ability to engage with Spanish-language media. Rather than pass up on a highly qualified candidate because Mark's Spanish proficiency wasn't up to the task, Pew hired a tutor and supported him on a learning odyssey. When he spoke about the ultimate success of language acquisition later in life, Mark highlighted that the interviews and media opportunities he was able to pursue in Spanish for work brought about a change in his personal life: conversations in Spanish with his mom. At first, his mom said he sounded like a *gringo* speaking Spanish, but Mark had his employer's financial support and the conviction to keep going with his Spanish tutor at Pew. Eventually, he was the one teaching her economics, demographics, and political jargon. He realized more fully through that experience how little formal instruction in Spanish his mom, a Chicana born in the L.A. area, had grown up with.

Having been both shamed for not speaking proficient Spanish and elevated for speaking technical Spanish related to work showed Mark, on a personal level, how language ideology acts upon individuals and communities.

Never Enough, By Design

As I went over the transcripts and audio of my interviews with Mark, Elaine, my siblings, and others who will be introduced in this text in later chapters, I began to feel something like grief. Not one of us had been allowed to feel like we were enough. While all of us took different paths, some fighting for respect, others for language acquisition, some focusing on other points of connection to our identities, and some giving up entirely, we had all felt the shame of being unable to claim our communities wholeheartedly. For some, the sting of teasing and insults became an impenetrable barrier to the language of our families, and for others, the lack of proficiency was used to question our authenticity. When interacting with Americans, people of the same background as us, and other people with Spanish-speaking backgrounds, nowhere was safe. We were never enough, no matter where we turned. Janet M. Fuller and Jennifer Leeman, authors of the book, *Speaking Spanish in the U.S.: The Sociopolitics of Language*, state:

> "For many Latinxs who don't speak Spanish, this comes with a sense of shame that has some similarity to the shame their parents or grandparents experienced if they did not speak English. However, it is often accompanied by a sense of loss, as well as feelings of cultural insecurity or inauthenticity. Indeed, the ideology that sees speaking Spanish as a requirement of 'authentic' Latinx identity is widespread among Latinxs as well as non-Latinxs ... linguistic insecurity can lead to avoidance, which in turn can contribute to language loss."

My sister Janet expressed this process of being mocked for early attempts and giving up, saying:

> "A few months ago, I had a conversation with *Titi* (Spanish diminutive for *tia* or aunt) Lizzy, and I said, 'You know what, I'm

just going to give up on trying to speak Spanish.' She said, 'Please don't, you should never give up.' I told her I'm 61 years old, and I've been around it; I've studied it. When I'm traveling by myself—I've been to Spain and to Peru—I can speak to strangers as best I can, and I don't get a glitch of insecurity. Still, it makes no sense to me why, at this point, I can't just speak it. The shame, the embarrassment, and the insecurity are so palpable. I can't do it. So I'm done."

I have wanted to give up; Janet wants to give up; and maybe you do, too? But where does that leave us?

The Tensions of a Latino Identity

In my broad-ranging conversation with Mark, he explained how his research uncovered discrepancies in how Latinos self-identify in the U.S.: relatively few survey respondents self-identified as Latino, while many more were more likely to consider themselves Mexican-American or Peruvian-American than Latino. This, for me, is a reminder that our pan-Latino identity in the U.S. is a complex construct. Although some believe it has been imposed on us by a hostile host, seeking assimilation as the final goal of our diasporic experiences, terms like "Hispanic" were implemented by the U.S. Census Bureau after years of organizing by Mexican, Puerto Rican, and Cuban civil rights groups looking for more accurate ways for people from Spanish-speaking communities to be officially counted. As Latinos, we represent a vast diversity of histories, cultures, traditions, ethnicities, and racial identities. It's no wonder many of us have struggled to adapt and present a palatable version of who we are to American society.

Garces-Conejos Blitvich notes that Spanish has become a "damned if you do, damned if you don't" problem for people like me, and maybe for you, too:

> "Latinidad is an identity in turmoil. In relation to the White majority, the outgroup Latinos are positioned as the other, racialised, and marginalised. The use of Spanish is discouraged, and English monolingualism is presented as the only path for the Latino minority to mainstream. On the other hand, within the Latino in-group, maintenance of Spanish is seen as a badge of honor and the only real claim to Latinidad. It is not difficult to see how this may lead to social and personal conflict since Latinos are trapped in a paradox in regards to the double standard applied to Spanish within their community/country."

These ideologies around language in the United States only widen the gap between who we think we are supposed to be and who we really are, leaving us with "this deep-rooted feeling of shame and identity fracture," according to Fuller and Leeman.

Taking our cues from the environment, we quickly learn that a lack of fluency in English will be socially penalized with lost opportunities, ostracization, and even violence. In my conversation with Mark, he reminded me that many Latino families still carry memories of institutional violence in the school system, perpetrated to force the Spanish-speaking children in attendance to only speak English. Fuller and Leeman explain this process further:

> "Adults and children alike are exposed to explicit and implicit societal messages that English is the key to fitting in and achieving success and that other languages are un-American and dangerous,

and these messages play a role in shaping household language practices and individual choices."

So there is a high cost to pay for not speaking English, and it dominates every space in society, from schools to workplaces, the media, and business. The opportunities to be immersed in Spanish are insufficient. From that context, we begin to buy into a collective ideology around the dominance and necessity of English, even as many of us are also exposed to ideologies about Spanish being an intrinsic and inalienable part of any Latino identity. And where do people like me, you, or Mark end up in all of this? We fall into the vast gulf left when the ideas that English is dominant and expedient and Spanish should just be "in our blood" are enacted upon us. The very hand that takes Spanish from us then points the finger at us for not speaking it.

Unpacking and divesting from these strongly held cultural beliefs and the shame they have left us with is intensely challenging work. Paola Ramos points out that language ideologies are built on lived experience, tribal attachment, and deeply rooted assumptions and ideas. These models "are formed in childhood and constantly reinforced throughout our lifetime." When the disconnect between the dominance of English and the expectation of Spanish, with insufficient support for its development, is repeated at every stage of our lives, it is all too easy for us to believe our whole identity is resting precariously on a deficit and to feel that this disconnect is our own fault.

CHAPTER FOUR

MEMORIES FROM THE ISLAND

"We don't come up with ideas about language completely on our own, in isolation from the world. Quite the opposite, people's beliefs about language (and other things) are shaped by our families and our communities, as well as the institutions and socio-economic and political structures with which we interact … When the standard language ideology portrays the way that the educated elite or dominant groups speak as better than other ways of speaking, this is not simply a neutral aesthetic preference; it reflects the higher status and power of the dominant group."

—*Speaking Spanish in the U.S.: The Sociopolitics of Language*, by Janet M. Fuller and Jennifer Leeman

I always say my first real trip to Puerto Rico happened when I was ten. I had been to the island as a toddler with my parents, but I retained no memories of that visit. This second visit became the foundation for my sense of the place where both my parents were born, the place many relatives still called home, and the deeper fissures in my sense of identity as a Puerto Rican kid who didn't speak Spanish.

My dad's older sister, my Titi Clara, brought me with her to Puerto Rico that summer. She lived in New Rochelle, Westchester County, and I occasionally spent weekends there as a kid. I loved visiting Titi Clara's lovely home and indulging in the rarest of treats: cable TV with HBO, watching movies and shows while raiding the well-stocked cookie jar during commercial breaks. It was on Titi Clara's TV that I first saw *Star Trek II: The Wrath of Khan* ("Khaaaaaan!") and a Robin Williams live stand-up special (zany!)

Dad posing with my beautiful aunts (L–R: Irma, Clara, Sonia, Isabel, Adel, Marianita, and Rita) at a birthday party. Irma and Clara's support was instrumental during my first "real" visit to PR.

When the plane touched down on the runway in San Juan, everyone started applauding. The relief and joy were palpable as fellow passengers smiled at each other, clapping and congratulating the pilot. People applauded as a way of expressing gratitude to the pilot and flight crew for getting them there safely, but there was an additional sense that arriving in Puerto Rico itself was a cause for celebration. The collective emotion, strangers hollering and applauding together, as the pilot announced, "Welcome to San Juan, Puerto Rico," was a revelation to me. I had "arrived" in the Caribbean.

On a recent trip I took to Grenada, the plane landed, and the flight attendant playfully reminded everyone to applaud. The moment of self-consciousness I felt reminded me of this small ritual of belonging that I had unlearned since my first flight at age ten with my aunt. Back then, I remember thinking, "What are they applauding for? Are they grateful we didn't crash?" Titi Clara must have explained that it was a way to thank the pilot and crew and celebrate being home. That early memory, combined with the reminder in Grenada, made me realize how powerful such simple acts of connection can be, marking home, culture, and the subtle ways we belong.

Americans in Puerto Rico

When I spoke to my five older siblings about their experiences with language growing up, a pattern emerged. I realized, through that conversation and others, that I was not the only kid who went to Puerto Rico for a visit later in childhood and was faced with the stark reality that my lack of Spanish, or lack of perfectly fluent Puerto Rican-accented Spanish, made me a foreigner in the place I had thought would embrace me in the way the United States never would.

Arriving in Puerto Rico, I had next to zero Spanish. I was nervous about it, but I knew I would be with my aunt, and I'd be able to lean on her. People spoke so quickly that the smattering of vocabulary I had was lost in a melody I could not grab hold of, and all I could say was *yo no puedo hablar español* or *yo hablo inglés solamente.* All I could manage was, "I can't speak Spanish" or "I only speak English," and not much else.

Lisa, my sister, told me she went to Puerto Rico as a child, visiting *El Yunque* (Puerto Rico's rainforest), but she was telling everyone she had gone to "yuca." The laughter confused her and made her question her ability to speak Spanish at all. Leslie, Lisa's twin, shared this feeling of coming from an English-speaking context and struggling to express herself, or of having to rely on relatives to translate.

Striking a pose at the San Felipe del Morro Fortress (El Morro) in Old San Juan. It was my introduction to the long and complicated history of Puerto Rico. Thanks, Jimmy!

My sister Yvonne described how, when she was around thirteen, she went to Puerto Rico to recover from an illness with her extended family.

Leaving the diaspora community in the U.S. and arriving on the archipelago, Yvonne described her experience:

"That's when I knew that there was something different, and that was Spanish, and the fact that we didn't speak it well. We don't speak it at all. Well, hardly much. We understood it, but we didn't really speak it. So that's my first recollection as far as, 'Oh, there's something different here.'"

Tony, my brother, remembers feeling confident, having been exposed to Spanish but never compelled to speak it, before everything changed one summer in Puerto Rico.

"There were thirteen of us kids that summer, and two Tonys: Tony Cubano and Tony Gringo. That's what they called me. But I was part of the group. I played basketball every night. I wasn't going to be left out. They tolerated me, but really it was more than that: we connected.

Still, when I tried to speak Spanish with my friends and messed it up, the shame hit hard. They laughed and goofed on me, and I thought, *Screw you, I'm only speaking to you in English now. You deal with me; you communicate with me.* But internally, I shut down. I closed that part off because I didn't want to take more risks and be shamed like that publicly."

Just as my mom had accidentally asked if a pineapple was "rape" instead of "ripe" and felt a stinging shame that was hard to shake, each of my siblings and I had memories of messing up in Spanish and internalizing a message about our capacity with the language of family. The difference for us was that we did not live in a Spanish-dominant place; in fact, all the pressure was on us to assimilate into the English world our parents had migrated to, so the shame quickly turned into a block that kept us from even trying. Where my mother had hardened her resolve to learn English that day in the grocery store, my brother Tony decided that he would stop trying to speak Spanish, and his passive bilingualism was all he would offer.

My sister Yvonne, while in Puerto Rico on a childhood visit, went to the hospital where her aunt lived. When the assembled group asked her what her favorite food was, she mispronounced the word for beans, *habichuelas,* instead saying something that sounded like a slang term for genitalia. She says,

> "And the whole floor lost it. They just lost their freaking minds. And I didn't know what I was saying at the moment, you know, but I knew it was something bad. And after that, you know, that's when I kind of shut down, like I didn't get with the whole, 'All right, I'm going to be really careful with my words.'"

I Am Boricua, Just So You Know!

I was clearly excited to be in this picture with rap legend DMC, actress Diane Neal, and superstar Rosie Perez. Rosie shared her story about language shame in her documentary, *Yo soy Boricua.*

Acclaimed actress Rosie Perez, known for her roles in *Do the Right Thing* and *Fearless*, directed a 2006 documentary called *Yo soy Boricua, pa' que tu lo sepas!* (I am Boricua, just so you know!) exploring the complexities of belonging and identity among Puerto Ricans living stateside, particularly in New York.

Rosie describes her own experience growing up in the documentary, saying:

> "My mother, she did not raise me, but the time that I did spend with her, visiting and spending weekends and what have you, she would only speak to us in English. She taught herself English, and she was very diligent in regard to having her children be Americans and having them have English as their first language rather than Spanish as their first language. My aunt would speak to me in Spanish all the time, and I would answer her in English. But it was difficult because when I would visit my mom, and I would speak Spanish to her, it would anger her or she would laugh at me because my pronunciation was incorrect or the grammar was incorrect or what have you, and it developed a lot of shame and humiliation in me."

Earlier in this chapter, we looked at a number of similar stories: my own, my siblings', and my mother's. The experience of making a mistake while learning a language and feeling shame seems nearly universal, but it is important to underline a difference.

When Rosie's mom or my mom experienced challenges learning English and were shamed for making mistakes, they did so in a context where they were learning a dominant, not a minority, language. This is an important distinction.

When my mom got made fun of for a mistake she made while learning English, she didn't give up, she doubled down and worked harder to get better. The choice to reject English as a means of avoiding shame and humiliation is one far fewer people make when it is the dominant language, as they often need it to function in the world. Although cruel and unnecessary, such teasing was sometimes effective motivation for first-generation migrants and immigrants, as their desire to avoid feeling that way again compelled them to redouble their efforts to learn.

But teasing works very differently for a minority language. Most people will step back and avoid it if they can because we naturally want to protect ourselves from shame. There is a difference between being teased in the majority language and being teased in the minority language. Teasing in the majority language can push the recipient of the humiliation toward English and toward fitting in with the dominant culture. Teasing in the minority language more often pushes you away from Spanish and away from that aspect of your heritage. Both are pressures to assimilate, but they operate differently.

Spanglish: Cuando la Vida Te Da Lemons, Make Limonada!

Spanglish is another example of super-syncretism, adaptation, and addition that we created in the United States. It reflects the in-between space of our lives: never quite enough for either side, yet it is a tool that allows us to navigate both. Spanglish lets migrant and immigrant kids go home and speak with *abuela* while also talking with their friends at school and on the block. It is a crucial adaptation, a skill set, a tool for survival, but we are often vilified for it because it is neither one thing nor the other. Spanglish, just like our features, is not easy to categorize or catalogue, and it defies assimilation, so it is seen as "other" and "less than."

Elisabet Velasquez, in an excerpt of a poem she wrote for MoMA, the Museum of Modern Art in New York, in collaboration with contemporary artist Papo Colo, described life as a Spanglish speaker like this:

> *My first heart is a complicated machine*
> *that breaks down in multiple languages.*
>
> *My first heart knows Spanish is a colonized tongue*
> *so she doesn't feel bad about speaking it terribly.*
>
> *My first heart knows English is a colonized tongue,*
> *so for fun, my first heart pisses off strangers by telling them*
>
> *"In America, we speak Spanglish."*
>
> *My first heart knows where she is from*
> *but still asks Puerto Rico for forgiveness for being born in Brooklyn.*[5]

Despite how common it is for Latinos in the U.S. to speak some version of Spanglish, we continue to struggle to make sense of its place in our lives and identities. When my sister Janet shared her story of visiting Puerto Rico as a child, she explained that she left New York thinking she was a pretty fluent Spanish speaker, only to realize that what she was speaking was, in fact, Spanglish.

"So I always thought that I was bilingual, which I guess I was in a sense. It was two languages—Spanglish and English. But then when I went to Puerto Rico, it was like, 'Oh, these Puerto Ricans speak different from the Puerto Ricans in the Bronx.' So I was kind of stuck in this place of, I don't speak your language. And everybody assumed I did. I felt like I missed something. How is it that they assume I do? How is it that there's a language they don't speak, which is Spanglish, and they don't speak English either? I was caught in that space."

---

[5] Elisabet Velasquez is a U.S.-born Puerto Rican writer and author of *When We Make It.* Papo Colo is a Puerto Rican artist who has been a key figure in the New York art scene since the 1970s.

We add creative new ways of communicating to the culture, even as we struggle to make ourselves understand, code-switch, and learn to navigate the multiple sources of linguistic pressure constantly bearing down on us. There are two sides to this coin, as, on one hand, we know Spanglish will never be considered "good enough." At the same time, on the other, there is pride in our ability to make lemonade out of lemons, build a new way of speaking out of the assimilative pressures, xenophobia, racism, and lack of support for our language in the U.S. It is a kind of joyful defiance for Latinos to create a linguistic system that allows us to live in two cultures. It is a way of adapting to being in-between yet. Still, you and I may see it for the crucial adaptation it is; Spanglish is more commonly vilified for being too ambiguous, too mixed up, too "like us."

Miguel Algarín, a Nuyorican poet from the Great Migration era and founder of the Nuyorican Cafe in the 1970s, described the birth of a new language in the context I come from in his book, *Nuyorican Poetry: An Anthology of Puerto Rican Words and Feelings:*

> "The experience of Puerto Ricans on the streets of New York has caused a new language to grow: Nuyorican. The Nuyoricans are a special experience in the immigration history of the city of New York ... There is at the edge of every empire a linguistic explosion that results from the many multilingual tribes that collect around wealth and power."

Turning Away from Spanish

Rather than becoming an opportunity for language acquisition, these stories of childhood visits to Puerto Rico show how our sense of identity had coalesced around English, or even coalesced around a deficit of Spanish, to a degree where we could no longer access the playful, flexible mindset that would have allowed us to make mistakes, grow, and learn as children visiting PR. I had the honor of interviewing Jennifer Leeman, in addition to reading her books and academic papers, in preparation for this project. She described what my siblings and I went through on those visits with depth and clarity, reminding me, and hopefully you, that the forces acting upon us were greater than just free will. Leeman told me:

> "...a huge part of it is also related to identity formation and the sense of 'this is who I am, and I'm connected to this language,' which adds to linguistic insecurity and a worry about making mistakes. There can be feelings of 'I'm not enough' or 'if I get this wrong, I'm an idiot' that make it harder for people who feel like they should already speak the language. Language learning is hard, and second-language learners also get embarrassed making mistakes, but it's not as tied to proving who they are."

In each of our stories, I am struck by how deeply we felt the shame and how quickly we were to turn our backs and stop even trying to speak Spanish, anything to avoid the embarrassment and pain of making a mistake in a language we were *supposed* to speak. What should have been opportunities to learn and practice, our visits to Puerto Rico quickly became the site of our realizations that we didn't really speak Spanish, we didn't really belong, and maybe we should even stop trying.

The power dynamics and interplay between Puerto Rico and our home in the United States left us, each in different ways, caught in the middle of a hurricane, leaving us unmoored and adrift. Even now, my sister Janet describes feeling disconnected from Latino networks, because her Spanish is not able to meet the expectations of those spaces. Meanwhile, in African American and white spaces, Janet feels very Latina. Nowhere can she feel like each piece that makes up her whole is embraced as an Afro-Latina woman who doesn't consider her Spanish proficient enough.

Assimilation: Did We Have a Choice?

As Jorell Meléndez-Badillo describes in his recent book, *Puerto Rico: A National History*, an asymmetrical relationship continues to exist between Puerto Rico and the United States, due to the archipelago's status as a territory of the U.S. Since acquiring Puerto Rico as a territory over a century ago, subsequent U.S. administrations have taken different approaches, at times forcing English-only education on the archipelago, and at other times leaving Puerto Ricans to retain Spanish education. For Puerto Ricans, including the diaspora, the issue of language is even more sensitive than for other Latinos, due to this unique relationship with the United States, with a power imbalance leaving Puerto Ricans at the whim of a Congress and president they don't even get to vote for.

In *The Sociopolitics of Multilingualism in the United States: The Intertwining of Language, Race, and Nation*, Jennifer Leeman elaborates on how the process of assimilation is enacted upon immigrants and migrants:

> "The objective of coercive assimilation was deculturation and domination, rather than structural integration. Language policies also were used to exercise and maintain power over enslaved Africans; teaching enslaved people to read or write was prohibited by law, and enslavers separated captives by language and forbade them from teaching their languages to their children in order to make resistance and rebellion more difficult."

We are stripped of the language and culture we brought and given nothing to fill the void. This is especially true for immigrants and migrants of color. No matter where we go, my siblings and I have to explain ourselves. We never get to be American in the U.S., but we are not Puerto Rican enough in Latino circles because we were not raised fluent in the language. Leeman points out that this void is less stark for immigrants of European descent, as linguistic assimilation offers the possibility of being incorporated into American whiteness. For my siblings and me, the very color of our skin prevents us from being incorporated, and we are left adrift, lost in the space between Puerto Rican, Black, and American.

Cocolo or Rockero?

My trip to Puerto Rico with my aunt at ten had two different phases. For the first week, we were in Guayama, moving back and forth between my mom's and my dad's families, even though I was visiting with my dad's sister. We stayed in the *caserío,* essentially Puerto Rico's version of the projects, born out of the mid-century redevelopment efforts that accompanied the push for emigration, all in service of Puerto Rico's industrial aspirations. My family was working class, not wealthy by any means, and they were among those who lived in the new housing developments.

At Titi Irma's, I spent part of the week with cousins on my maternal side, as well as some neighborhood kids who spoke only Spanish. I don't remember their names, but I remember playing with them, riding the Ferris wheel at the local carnival, and struggling to communicate. I spoke in English, they spoke in Spanish, and somehow we managed.

Down the street lived my mother's sister Carmen and her children. Carmen spoke only Spanish, but her kids, Yadira, Indira, Greta, Ivia, and Edward, had learned English in school.

The strange fluctuations in English education across the archipelago, a result of U.S. imperialism, were evident in the divergent levels of English proficiency I encountered on this trip. This was the mid-1980s, so American pop music was all the rage with most kids and teenagers. My cousins and I bonded over Michael Jackson and Journey as much as anything else. That made our connection easy, familiar, and fun. Unbeknownst to me at the time, I had stepped into the fertile, contentious divide between the *cocolos* and *rockeros*. *Cocolos* represented the members of that generation who were interested in Caribbean and Latin music, while the *Rockeros* were hungry for the rock hits coming out of the U.S.

The cousins on my mom's side were a godsend during that trip. They all spoke English, and while I was in Guayama, we bonded over music and pop culture. L–R: Indira, Ivia, Yadira, and Roxanne.

It turns out, I had unknowingly been thrust into a cauldron of cultural change in Puerto Rico and other Caribbean countries as musical traditions had become markers of race and class differences. According to Frances Aparicio in her book *Listening to Salsa: Gender, Popular Music, and Puerto Rican Cultures*, a growing divide emerged in musical taste among Puerto Rican youth in the 1980s. *Cocolos*, an African-derived term, referred to young black men who could be found at Salsa concerts or blasting Salsa from the speakers of their beat-up old cars, and *rockeros* were white, upper and middle class young Puerto Ricans who preferred to listen to rock music, most of it coming out of the U.S. I arrived ready to share the songs I was obsessing over on the radio in the U.S., Michael Jackson, Journey, and more, but the Salsa that had always been background noise to me began to take on a new light while I was on the island.

It was in this context that I first discovered Rubén Blades, a Panamanian musician, singer, and songwriter who was not only behind some of the biggest hits of the *Salsa Dura* era, including "El Cantante," which became a massive hit for Héctor Lavoe, defining his career, but also starred in films and put out his own albums.

My aunt had a record player, and I spent many hours on that visit spinning records from her collection of mostly Salsa. I found an album with a striking cover in which seven men posed shirtless, lit in blue and deep shadows as they looked up with intense emotion toward the album title. Behind them, there seemed to be a blood-red sunrise illuminating the background. The recently released album was *Buscando América* (Searching for America) by Rubén Blades y El Seis del Solar. I put on the record and lowered the needle, immediately intrigued by what I was hearing. As I flipped through the album notes, something else caught my attention. This album included English translations of all of the lyrics. I hungrily devoured each song, running my finger under the English words on the page as I listened to Ruben's voice singing them from the record player. Suddenly, what had been lush, beautifully arranged, and layered music became so much more. Blades's lyrics spoke of the harsh realities in Latin American countries facing foreign interference, dictatorships, civil wars, and poverty. When he called out for *América,* he didn't mean the United States; he meant the land stretching from the Rio Grande to Patagonia, calling for freedom, dignity, and strength in our identities despite having been "kidnapped" by foreign powers.

When I arrived in Puerto Rico on this first real visit, I identified culturally as American. It was exciting to find common ground with cousins and neighbors who shared my love of American music, especially if they could speak enough English for us to chat about it. Yet, it was as though the soundscape of the first decade of my life suddenly began to find moments to break through and escape the background, entering the forefront of my consciousness. Salsa was the music my parents so often had on in the house, the music I heard at parties and events, the music I had always seen as my father and mother's thing. But something had already begun to shift, and although I arrived in Puerto Rico firmly identified with the rockers, I eventually came to a place where I found myself in both camps. I am today firmly and unabashedly both a *cocolo* and a *rockero*, because I love Van Halen as much as I do El Gran Combo.

But it wasn't time to return to New York just yet, and the visit to Puerto Rico both highlighted the ways I did not feel I belonged and planted the seeds of what would eventually become my journey to wholeness.

It was the next week, visiting my grandpa, when I really began to feel the strange, uneasy grief of not speaking the language of my own family.

CHAPTER FIVE

ABUELO'S HOUSE

"Language is the vehicle for memory—collective and individual. It is the site of practices, ideas, and stories that make *us* a *we*. It is also the site of practices, ideas, and stories that make us an I."
—*Household Perspectives on Minority Language Maintenance and Loss: Language in the Small Spaces*, by Isabel Velázquez

After staying with Titi Irma, I spent a few days with my abuelo (grandfather) Ismael in his house. It was not easy. He spoke no English, and I did not yet have the Spanish to bridge the gap. He was happy to have me there, and I was glad to see him, but we had no real way of connecting. After the high of running around the neighborhood with kids my age in Guayama, landing in this quiet, humble, old-fashioned house with an older man I could not speak to was jarring. I know Titi Clara and the other adults planning the trip for me were aware we would have a language barrier, and that Abuelo's house was not very kid-centric in that era of his life, but still, it was the right thing to do. You paid respect to your elders, and visiting your grandfather was part of that.

The house was modest but comfortable enough. What I remember most are the walks to the local store in the mornings. Puerto Rico's bakeries are a thing of beauty, with warm, fresh bread served with butter and coffee. It was there that I first discovered the *media noche* sandwich. It looked a little like a Cuban, but simpler, with ham and cheese pressed inside soft, sweet bread that melted in your mouth. I had never had anything like it before. Growing up in New York, I knew bacon, egg, and cheese sandwiches, but this was another world.

This is my only picture with Abuelo Ismael, taken during that trip to his home in Salinas when I was ten. I loved seeing him, but it was a difficult few days, as we couldn't talk to each other much.

Those days passed slowly. I would grab a sandwich or some candy, wander the neighborhood, and watch the local, Spanish-only TV stations that my abuelo had. There was a kind of silence neither of us knew how to fill. Still, I knew, even then, that this time with my father's father, the man who gave me my last name, the man who migrated to New York looking for work in factories and then went back to San Felípe to live out his days, leaving constellations of family behind in the United States, was important. That short visit grounded me in another piece of my family's story, one that felt less like an adventure and more like obligation, but no less important.

Sugarcane and Factories

Salinas is a fishing town. Within this town is Aguirre, where a massive sugarcane plant once stood. I remember hearing that my grandfather might have worked there for a while, maybe even my father, too. Like the *caserío* in Guayama, Salinas had its poorer section, San Felipe. But my grandfather owned a modest house and a little property there. Home ownership gave him some stability, even if the neighborhood itself wasn't much to talk about.

Born in 1913 in Guayama to Tiburcio López and Maria Anita Pica de López, Abuelo Ismael was raised during the first decades of United States rule in Puerto Rico. In 1898, the United States "acquired" the archipelago from Spain. The people, like my great-grandparents and grandparents, who were laboring in sugar plantations, working the land, fishing the seas, and feeding their families as well as the empire with the sweat of their brows, were transferred from one colonial power to another. According to census records, my great-grandfather, Tiburcio, born in 1876, was a foreman on a sugar plantation, while my great-grandmother, Maria Anita, sadly lived as an enslaved person on Hacienda Pica in Guayama.[6]

An image of my great-grandfather, Tiburcio López. Born in 1876, he was a foreman on a sugar plantation.

Showing clearly how colonization has been a throughline, creating the conditions we see today for Puerto Ricans, including my family and me, Meléndez-Badillo writes:

"We cannot understand Puerto Rico's current fiscal, political, and social crises without recognizing its colonial reality. To cast light on Puerto Rico's current moment, we must acknowledge colonialism without overlooking vibrant histories of indigenous

---

[6] I'm deeply grateful to my brother, Tony, for these details about our ancestors. Tony has long served as our unofficial family historian and archivist.

resistance and maroon communities to nationalist insurrections and massive mobilizations that demanded the resignation of corrupt elected officials."

Unlike my visit with Abuelo Ismael, I was able to converse with my mom's dad, Abuelo Juan, during my visit to PR. His years in the armed forces offered him the opportunity to practice speaking English.

At the center of all this was a massive push to get Puerto Ricans off the island and into northeastern U.S. cities. In his essay, "The Puerto Rican Diaspora," historian Adalberto López explains the labor needs behind this migration:

> "It was the chronic lack of employment on the island on one hand and the demand on the mainland for cheap unskilled or semi-skilled labor in the competitive industries (such as the garment industry) and the 'service' sector (janitors, dishwashers, hotel maids, busboys, etc.) on the other that accounted primarily for

the beginning of a massive migration of Puerto Ricans to the continental United States in the 1940s."

My grandfather, I began to understand, although I lacked the information and wisdom to fully grasp the situation at ten years of age, grew up and formed his own family, bringing my aunts and father into the world with my grandmother, who then predeceased him by several decades, under the boot of colonial rule. When my dad was a teenager, Abuelo came with him to New York for the first time, joining one of my aunts and looking for work in the factories that were hiring Puerto Rican laborers during the post-war economic boom and the Great Migration. But people like my grandfather and dad were supposed to stay quiet, stay small, keep their heads down, and work the jobs other Americans did not want to work.

This power dynamic plays a role on the archipelago as well. As Meléndez-Badillo describes it, the Americans saw educating and forcing assimilation upon the local population of the Caribbean islands they had just acquired as the obvious and desired outcome for Puerto Rico, or "Porto Rico" as Anglophones called it in the early years:

"As the United States acquired new territories after the war of 1898, a debate ensued in Washington about how to deal with the people living in those territories. The so-called white man's burden was to educate Puerto Ricans in Anglo-Saxon traditions, which was part of a broader colonial project. Native communities had been forcefully and violently assimilated through a system of boarding schools; Hawai'i, the Philippines, and Cuba also proved to be testing grounds for formulas to promote and enforce Americanization ... Education was considered an instrument for the assimilation of Puerto Ricans."

As my father and grandfather were pushed stateside by politicians seeking to reduce the population of Puerto Rico and disperse low-wage workers into the economy in the continental U.S., the forces of assimilation were bearing down on them, on our family, from all sides.

You're in the United States. Speak English.

Language has always been a powerful tool for subjugation, and the maintenance or loss of Spanish for Puerto Ricans, or, indeed, most migrants, takes place in a context wherein the colonial project finds insidious and overt ways to push for assimilation. This is complicated by our brown skin, our features that cannot be neatly folded into whiteness, as soon as our accents no longer prevent us from passing as just another white American. The goal, for immigrants and migrants of color like my family and me, seems to be less assimilation and more a facsimile of assimilation that seeks to keep us in our place at the bottom of the food chain, rather than force integration, since we were always too "dark" for that anyway.

It is no accident that I have felt my entire life like I am strung out between the facets of my identity, struggling to make something whole out of pieces I am relentlessly told don't go together. And, despite the reality that "language is part of a broader power struggle which is mostly fought through discourses around language," as stated by Isabel Velázquez in her book, *Household Perspectives on Minority Language Maintenance and Loss: Language in the Small Spaces*, I took on the shame of not speaking Spanish, as did my siblings, as if it were our own personal failing.

Bilingualism was not always seen as an asset, leading many of our parents to deprioritize Spanish. Not seeing how their decisions played into the hands of the social forces acting upon them, many of our parents decided that it was better for us to be English speakers than bilingual.

Any trace of an accent was a liability they knew all too well, and it was hard for them to see the benefit of speaking Spanish.

And yet, there I was, at ten, unable to communicate with my own grandfather, leaving us to watch TV I didn't understand in silence together in his humble house with its cool, cement floors on hot summer days in PR. According to Elaine Allard, Katherine Mortimer, Sarah Gallo, Holly Link, and Stanton Wortham in "Immigrant Spanish as Liability or Asset? Generational Diversity in Language Ideologies at School":

> "Language ideologies establish connections between language and people, connections that have implications about who people are, what they are worth, and how they should be treated."

The norm in the United States, especially in the 1970s and 1980s when I was growing up in the Bronx, was monoglossic, or one language only. According to Elaine Allard and her colleagues, as quoted above, the norm of monolingualism is so entrenched in the United States that language becomes divorced from its social context, unable to cast languages as disembodied systems. "The speech of many Latino students, in which students *translanguage*, [italics mine] moving fluidly between two or more linguistic codes to serve their communicative purposes, are often seen as deficient because they do not adhere to 'native standards' of English or 'foreign standards' of Spanish," the paper continues, affirming and giving words to feelings I have carried with me since early childhood.

I am beginning to understand why it was never enough, no matter what I did.

No wonder I have felt mixed up. As Allard et al. explain, "most U.S. schools operate under monoglossic ideologies of language and language ideologies establish links between language and people. Latinos have often been viewed as mixed-up people whose speech departs from monolingual norms." For many migrants and immigrants, no matter what they do or which language they speak, they are always viewed as something mixed up, confused, irregular, and even worthy of distrust. In my case, my ability to speak English was never going to be a problem in U.S. culture. However, my inability to speak Spanish left me with a sense of alienation from my Puerto Rican culture. I was in the United States, speaking English, as was expected, yet left with an enormous sense of grief and loss.

Becoming Nuyorican

As part of its 2000 series *Ethnic New York*, WNET produced the documentary *Nuyoricans: Puerto Ricans in New York*. I was thrilled to make an appearance in it.

And yet, despite all of the pressure, the poverty, the hard labor, xenophobia, and double standards placed upon our migrant communities, we continued to find ways to not only survive but flourish and add incredible benefits to our new home. In New York, in particular, diaspora communities came together and forged new cultures, languages, and ways of being, with awe-inspiring creativity, resilience, and joy. We reclaimed what was forced upon us as a badge of shame and a marker of low class, and we turned all of it into something beautiful: Nuyorican culture. Monica Brown writes in "Neither Here Nor There: Nuyorican Literature, Home, and the 'American' National Symbolic":

"The term 'Nuyorican' has had shifting historical connotations, both negative and positive. Along with the more 'geographically inclusive' term 'Neorican,' it has been used pejoratively by islanders and others as a way to describe those living in the 'north.' However, these terms have also been used as markers of national pride."

We demonstrated through our joyful cultural expressions, unique accents and ways of speaking, and our use of Spanglish, that Puerto Ricans were not going to quietly bow our heads under the boot of empire, as Monica Brown attests in her work. We made every facet of our lives a poem to our own dignity, exposing the myth of the American Dream and denouncing the challenging conditions we were exposed to, be it under the control of Spain, under the control of the U.S. on the island, or in the United States.

My embrace of the term "Nuyorican" is not a rejection of other important and even essential identity markers, like Puerto Rican or Boricua. It is an acknowledgment of the contributions many stateside Puerto Ricans have made as they created lives and livelihoods in New York and other parts of the northeastern and midwestern United States. This psychological and emotional exercise in identity formation has included all aspects of our culture, music, food, language, and more, to claim our own spaces in a land many of my forebears were forced to inhabit.

I was proud to represent the youth leadership organization Muevete in the PBS production *Nuyoricans*.

Abuelo's Funeral in Salinas

The year was 1998. I was in my second year at the Upper Manhattan Empowerment Zone, a government-funded nonprofit organization tasked with stimulating economic development activity in the neighborhoods of East, Central, and West Harlem, Washington Heights, and Inwood. I was still very much on an upward curve in my public relations career when I got the call that my grandfather had died. There had been a fire in his house, and he was trapped inside. I do not know the exact details now. Maybe he was disoriented at an advanced age; maybe he could not unlock a door. The facts have blurred over time. What I do remember is the shock and a look I had never seen before on my dad's face. My grandfather was 85, still a strong, independent man even at that age, the rare kind of man who outlived his wife by several decades, caring for himself and standing on his own until the last.

My grandfather had lived a life of labor—working the sugar fields, in factories, boxing, playing music, and raising a large family of daughters and one son, my dad, who would later come north. Irma was the first to move to New York, then my grandfather, then my father, and the rest. They settled in East Harlem, known by the New York Latino community as *El Barrio*, and eventually, many of us ended up in the Bronx. Eventually, my grandfather made his way back to the house in Salinas. Having spent years working in the United States, he could finally retire.

My grandfather was the only grandparent I had extended contact with. The others were either gone or distant, and that scarcity made his presence all the more important and his loss all the harder to bear. After the trip to Puerto Rico when I was ten, we went back again for Christmas the following year, and my grandfather came to stay with my dad and me not long after my parents' separation, when I was a freshman in college. The language barrier between us never stopped getting in the way, but I felt a deep sense of familial connection with my abuelo despite it.

When I went to the funeral, I was one of the pallbearers along with my cousins. When a family member asked me to say a few words in the cemetery as the coffin was prepared at the side of our family plot, I had to dig deep inside myself to rise to the occasion. Words. It was the words that were missing in my memories of my abuelo, but I resolved to say something in English—there were very few or no family members left who would not understand English by then—and then to say some words in Spanish, a token of love for my grandfather.

The heat was stifling, and sweat lined my brow as I prepared to speak. I remember choosing a scripture from the Book of Ecclesiastes, something that illustrated the paradox of honoring a life through mourning felt right. While we are born as a blank slate in many ways, my grandfather left this world with a legacy worthy of celebration behind him.

> *A good name is better than fine perfume,*
> *and the day of death, better than the day of birth.*
> *It is better to go to a house of mourning*
> *than to go to a house of feasting.*
> —Ecclesiastes 7:1, 2a

I wanted to say part of it in Spanish to honor him and the place, but I didn't have much time to prepare. By then, I had some basic Spanish from high school, and I asked an aunt to help. Between the two of us, we made a rough translation of the section of Ecclesiastes I wanted to share.

> *Un buen nombre es mejor que un buen aroma,*
> *y el día de la muerte es mejor que el día del*
> *nacimiento. Es mejor ir a una casa donde hay*
> *tristeza que ir a una casa con mucha comida.*

Go ahead. Put it through Google Translate. It's not a good translation of the verse, but it was what I was able to come up with at the time, and I was grateful for my ability to do so.

Speaking Spanish to a group makes me very conscious of every word. My heart beat in my throat, my voice felt strained, and I found myself looking up and to the left as I searched for words. When I am nervous about speaking Spanish, I almost feel as if I were lying. The process in my brain triggers a deep feeling of inauthenticity in me, even as I am striving with all my might to connect to my own roots. I do not remember the exact order of English and Spanish that I used. What I do remember is that I spoke deliberately, that people listened, and that afterward they told me how much they appreciated it. No one mocked me. It was sincere, and it mattered.

At the repast, we all shared stories about Abuelo. It was a multigenerational affair with both English and Spanish. Aunts and other older family members spoke Spanish or switched back and forth, while younger generations tended to speak more English.

Although the occasion of Abuelo's funeral was a sad reason to come together, I was grateful for the opportunity to explore the areas where my family grew up, like here in Aguirre.

My cousin Jaime, affectionately known as Jimmy, took us on a tour of Aguirre, the next town over from Salinas, where we encountered abandoned sugarcane processing plants. It was like walking through a time capsule, seeing the Puerto Rico of my parents and grandparents. The same cousin, Jimmy, took me on a beautiful tour of Viejo San Juan and La Fortaleza fourteen years earlier, when I was ten, sparking my curiosity and admiration for the island and its history. This trip, made for very sad and tragic reasons, became a beautiful, full-circle moment for me and my relationship to Puerto Rico.

In the end, those visits, three solid memories of time spent with my grandfather, were what I was left with. It was enough to feel a solid grounding in who I am and the kind of people we are—humble, hardworking, fun-loving, and effusive, but each memory was mediated by my limited Spanish. I am someone who asks questions and wants stories, and the language barrier turned many of those questions into missed opportunities. The stories I never got to hear and the connection we could not forge, even as we sat together in the same rooms, is its own kind of grief.

A longtime friend from elementary school, Alma McKinley, shared a similar story of returning to Puerto Rico for several funerals and having meaningful connections with family that brought her a different sense of life on the archipelago:

"It almost felt like if my family could have had an Irish wake, they would have. In an Irish wake, the body comes home after it is embalmed, and the wake happens right there in the house. People gather, eat sandwiches, drink beer, and talk over the coffin in the living room. And honestly, that was the vibe of a Puerto Rican wake. My aunt did not have more than a third-grade education, but she was the first matriarch to pass, and when she died, it was like a presidential funeral. We left her small town in Naranjito, came down the mountains, and headed toward the cemetery in Bayamon, a busy city with real traffic. We had police escorts the whole way. My mother was so impressed. She kept saying, 'If only Titi Laura could see this.'

The next year, we visited for my Uncle Miguel's funeral, the darkest-skinned in the family, so much so that everyone called him *Negro*, a name used with love, not insult, even though I later learned more about colorism, racism, and white supremacy. I began questioning that language with my mother. My aunts and uncles were a full rainbow from fair to dark, and Miguel stood out not just for his complexion but for his work in agriculture and the way he always brought us huge, freshly cut bushels of bananas and plantains when we visited from New York. Once, he took us on a ride through an area so impoverished that 'poverty-stricken' did not even begin to describe it, driving a black SUV loaded with boxes of local fruit. After a long drive, we reached a dirt road lined with tin shacks, and a frail man in a stained white shirt and rope-tied pants came out to greet him like an old friend. Only then did I realize that Miguel was making deliveries, quietly giving back in the way everyone in my family seemed to do. That memory stayed with me for years, and when Hurricane Maria devastated the island, I could not stop thinking about that man in the tin shack and how completely the storm must have swallowed everything around him."

What I find fascinating about these funeral experiences in Puerto Rico is that, for both Alma and me, we were able to find true meaning in what it meant to be Puerto Rican, despite our limited ability to speak Spanish. That culture is transmitted in so many more ways than language. It can even be transmitted through how we mourn and how we express generosity.

CHAPTER SIX

JE M'APPELLE ROBERT: LEARNING FRENCH IN THE BRONX

"French was required. Its lingering elite prestige goes back almost a thousand years, when a small group of Norman French speakers conquered a large group of diversely dialected Old English speakers ... Century after century, Middle and Modern English were continually forged through French, including not only words like *elite* and *prestige*, but *lake, mountain, flower,* and thousands of others which now seem impeccably English. Like many English speakers, I heard both the elegance and arrogance in the roll of French uvular /r/ or a cascade of nasal vowels."

—*Language City: The Fight to Preserve Endangered Mother Tongues in New York*, by Ross Perlin

Translation, Not Language Acquisition

I don't know at what point exactly my parents accepted, and I, along with them, that I would not speak Spanish. It's hard to remember something that never happened, the language that stayed in the soundtrack. But even as I had internalized my parents' shame and struggle, stemming from the xenophobia and racism they faced as migrants for their lack of proficiency in English, and received negative messages about Spanish from the environment I grew up in, I still longed to understand and be understood in the language of my family. The few memories I have, such as the one I shared earlier of my father teaching me how to pronounce scripture, serve as a source of clarity for me. I did not reject this language, and I did not fail at it somehow because of a flaw in my character or some essential lack of the Puerto Rican-ness. The language was taken from me by the forces of assimilation in the U.S. mainland.

Another memory I cherish of approaching Spanish growing up happened in the 1980s when I was a preteen. A Salsa song became a huge hit: "Lluvia" by Eddie Santiago. I'm sure we didn't own the album, so it must have been playing on Spanish radio. My mother was probably listening to it one particular day when the song caught my ear.

It was on this old-timey stereo set that I first heard the song "Lluvia" by Eddie Santiago. I also clearly went through an emo phase. Note the 8-track and VHS cassettes!

"Lluvia" belongs to the genre known as *Salsa Romántica*, a softer, pop-infused style that emerged in the 1980s. Along with Lalo Rodríguez's "Devórame Otra Vez," it is considered one of the defining songs of that period. For Salsa purists, *Salsa Romántica* was a letdown. The 1970s had been the era of *Salsa Dura*, music rooted in the community and engaged with its struggles and social issues. Salsa in this period was also defined by a brassy, aggressive, and irresistible sound as dance music. By the 1980s, the music had shifted toward love songs, softer themes, and broader commercial appeal. But to me, "Lluvia" was simply beautiful.

At the time, I only knew the word *lluvia* meant rain. There were a few other scattered words I could recognize, but I had no real sense of what the song was about. It was the melody that drew me in first. I was intrigued and asked my mother to explain the lyrics. Patiently, she walked me through each verse, and it turned out the song was less about love than about falling out of it. A heartbreak song. The singer described kisses as cold as rain.

That moment of translation, of decoding the song together, became a meaningful connection between us. I was romantic, impressionable, and hungry to understand the song I had fallen in love with, and basking in a moment where I felt like a little boy again, able to be curious and have my mother guide me. I wanted to learn, but I felt more comfortable asking for a translation than trying to pronounce and memorize the words myself.

But even as I learned the words and traced their meanings over the melodies I loved so much, I felt the raw sting of loss. If I needed to have songs translated for me, were they really mine?

Je M'Appelle Robert

I was honored to be invited back years later as a graduation speaker. By then, it was no longer J.H.S. 80, but Middle School 80. Years after this, I would return as a teaching artist.

It is ironic, almost bitterly so, to me to this day that it was French, not Spanish, that we were expected to learn at my junior high school, J.H.S. 80, in the Bronx. French was presented to us as a clean, posh, and upwardly mobile option, even a language that would help us stand out and prove our intelligence. In junior high, now called middle school in most places, I was enrolled in a Special Progress (SP) class that allowed me to move from seventh to ninth grade, skipping grade eight entirely. This program came with a set schedule of classes, including French. This was seen as prestigious, a sign of our perceived ability to handle a language class with a greater degree of difficulty. There were those who studied French and those who studied Spanish, was the message we received.

My SP classmates from J.H.S. 80 on a trip to the Metropolitan Museum of Art. In addition to skipping eighth grade, we had the privilege (?) of taking French in ninth grade.

Our French teacher was named Ms. Wisotsky, and I remember her clearly. On the first day of class, she had each of us introduce ourselves. If our names didn't roll easily off the French tongue, she assigned us French versions of our names. In ninth-grade French, I was no longer Rodney, but Robert, pronounced "Ro-bear." While I can see a potential pedagogical argument for this, the disconnect with the realities of language and identity for a class of mostly Puerto Rican kids in the Bronx who were now being given new, more European names is stark. Why not teach us how to say our own names in French instead of replacing them?

But there I was, Robert. Every time I raised my hand, Ms. Wisotsky's reply was, "Oui, Robert?" It became my classroom identity. Some of the other students got to keep their names if the teacher felt they were easily pronounced in French, but mine, she decided, didn't fit. Even more ironically, I have a brother named Robert, so there I was, a Bronx kid in French class, living for a year under my brother's name because mine wouldn't do.

Although I did not see it at the time, it is now hard not to see the message buried in that symbolic move to rename me. What does it mean to tell a room full of Brown and Black kids that they can't be in this Special Progress class and keep their own names?

I loved school and enjoyed pushing myself academically, so I gave little thought to the vast difference in the importance placed on French versus Spanish at my school. I put in the effort, doing flash cards and drills to memorize vocabulary and verb conjugations, even though, in the back of my mind, I did think, "Sure, maybe I'll use this someday. But probably never."

So there we were, a class full of mostly Puerto Rican kids in the Bronx, learning to count, make basic conversation, and conjugate verbs in French.

At the time, I didn't question the experience much. Over time, I have begun to see how the education system's bias against Spanish, seeing it as a marker of poverty, otherness, and the browning of America, pushed me to study this language that had little utility and no resonance for me, while I was wholly unsupported with the language that I was missing.

Spanish is an American Language

Spanish plays a huge role in the United States. Not only do around 45 million people speak Spanish at home in the U.S. today, according to Mark Hugo López and the Pew Research Center, but the language has deep historic roots in our country. From Puerto Rico to Los Angeles, the United States acquired vast swaths of former Spanish colonies as a result of armed conflicts in the 19th century. Along with Texas,

Arizona, California, and Puerto Rico, to name a few, came the Spanish language and Spanish speakers.

Adding to this, later waves of migration and immigration, such as the one that brought my parents to New York, saw millions of people from every corner of Latin America make the U.S. their home, enriching it with our language, culture, and hard work.

Through my discussions and research, it became clearer to me than ever that the negative narrative surrounding bilingualism is rooted not in science but in politics and history. From the beginning, America has used language as a tool of control. Native peoples, Indigenous communities, and African people were stripped of their languages and cultures in order to assimilate them and make them more manageable within the dominant society. Public education, as it was established in this country, was designed with assimilation in mind, not pluralism.

At the same time, there has always been a bilingual education movement in the United States, though it has historically faced opposition. Elaine shared with me an example she uncovered in her research: German-speaking immigrants became targets of growing distrust during WWI, and restrictive backlash against bilingualism resulted from that period of hyper-nationalistic hostility toward immigrant communities.

If even white immigrants like Germans faced this type of negative response for bilingualism and bore the brunt of intense pressure to assimilate, the pressure was even greater on communities of color. By the 1950s and 1960s, large numbers of Cubans were arriving in Miami, precipitating the first bilingual education program in the country in 1963 in Miami-Dade. The same Mexicans who had been invited to support the U.S. during WWII with the *braceros* program, promoted to find workers who could replace the many men serving overseas and sustain the American economy during the war, began putting down roots and shifting from temporary migration to immigration.[7] Around the same time, Puerto Rican migration increased with "Operation Bootstrap," the economic development program designed to modernize the island's economy and attract U.S. investment. Later waves of immigration from Central and Latin America, the Dominican Republic, Haiti, and parts of West Africa contributed to a shift from predominantly white immigration patterns to the increased visibility of Black and Brown newcomers.

As the demographics of immigration changed, so too did the response. Anti-immigrant sentiment increased as America faced an influx of immigrants of color. Bias and racism began to undergird much of the opposition to bilingual education, and these forces continue to shape the narrative today.

The "browning of America" is what most deeply unsettles those who advocate for nativist, English-only, and ultimately white supremacist aims, even when those aims are disguised with academic language or euphemisms. There is a clear historical narrative that runs from the treatment of Indigenous peoples through all of the waves of immigration: an ongoing impulse, reflected in educational and social policy, to enforce assimilation.

At its core, the very idea of American nationhood has functioned as an assimilationist project. One of the most powerful tools in that project has been the public education system. Although proponents of bilingual

---

[7] "From 1942 to 1964, millions of migrant workers crossed the border from Mexico into the United States as *braceros*, a Spanish word for "laborer who works with his arms." The Bracero Program was a federally sponsored labor program that was initiated following negotiations with the U.S. and Mexican governments. Officially called the Mexican Farm Labor Program, it was created to address the U.S. labor shortage caused by World War II and lasted from 1942 to 1964. It brought migrants, mainly men, to the United States from Mexico to work seasonally, on short-term contracts. The National Archives. https://prologue.blogs.archives.gov/2023/09/27/the-bracero-program-prelude-to-cesar-chavez-and-the-farm-worker-movement/

education have often sought to move the United States toward a more inclusive model—one that echoes the European framework in which multilingualism is not stigmatized but accepted—the reality has been different. In much of Europe, for example, speaking multiple languages is common and uncontroversial. In the United States, however, bilingualism has often been treated with suspicion, even hostility.

When bilingualism or multilingualism has been acknowledged in legislation and policy, it has largely been in the service of assimilation. The goal has been less about fostering genuine bilingualism than about accelerating English proficiency. In practice, bilingual education in the United States has often been about producing better English speakers rather than nurturing truly bilingual students.

Fighting for True Bilingual Education in the U.S.

As I began to understand the role that a lack of community and institutional support for Spanish played in my monolingual status, I wanted to learn more about bilingual education. My conversation with Dr. Elaine Ruiz-López, CEO of the International Leadership Charter School, bestselling author, and my sister-in-law, shed light on the topic.

Looking back to the 1970s, Elaine explained how bilingual programs began to emerge in New York, but their intentions may not have been what you would expect. Instead of promoting bilingualism, the premise was to educate students in Spanish to speed their transition to learning their second language: English. Some models did have as a goal the maintenance of the minority language, and others focused on additional language learning. In academic circles and the bilingual education community, there was a shift toward acknowledging that preserving the native language was a valuable goal alongside English as an additional language. Of course, none of these models took into account kids like me who were not able to receive sufficient input of our heritage language at home and would have benefited from bilingual education to help us preserve our language, culture, and identity.

In the 1990s, bilingual education took another leap forward with the advent of dual-language immersion programs, Elaine said. This expanded the scope beyond grammar drills and actually saw students spending half their educational time learning in Spanish. I dearly wish I had had access to something like this, and I believe our inability to see Spanish as an American language has limited the rollout of such programs. While we are loudly expected to speak Spanish as Latinos, we are quietly expected to have thoroughly lost it by the third generation in the United States.

In fact, I was reminded by a poignant story highlighted in Jennifer Leeman's work, "The Sociopolitics of Multilingualism in the United States: The intertwining of Language, Race and Nation." In 1974, the case of *Lau v. Nichols* made its way to the Supreme Court, marking a change in the way we view bilingual education in the U.S. The case focused on San Francisco public schools' provision of education in English only, with no support for children of Chinese ancestry with limited English proficiency in the school system. The findings demonstrated that excluding these children from meaningful participation due to their lack of English proficiency, which stemmed directly from their national origin, qualified as a violation of the Civil Rights Act. This court ruling, which happened to come down in the same year I was born, sparked growth in bilingual programs and increased federal funding.

It is important to note that even in *Lau v. Nichols*, we still see a paradigm in which bilingual education is treated as a stepping stone to English for children who lack the proficiency to learn in that language. I have to wonder whether a rights-based framework could have been applied to me, and whether bilingual education had been designed to preserve and enhance Spanish. As Puerto Ricans, my parents were born American citizens as a result of the 1917 Jones Act, and I dream of a world where our right to be a Spanish-speaking family, even on the mainland, could have been recognized.

In the years that have followed my experience having French promoted as the more valuable language to learn, even in the Bronx, things have changed, but we do have a long way to go. Fuller and Leeman describe the resistance to viewing Spanish as a valuable asset in their book, *Speaking Spanish in the U.S.: The Sociopolitics of Language*, writing, "Sometimes Spanish is framed as valuable for future employment opportunities, but more commonly it is seen as important for ethnoracial identity and/or necessary for familial communication either in the U.S. or with relatives abroad."

Reimagining a Bilingual Future

Asking what might have made the difference for me is a powerful exercise. Rather than building resentment, it helps me to see the bigger picture, release shame, and dream of a future where bilingualism is truly supported for families like mine. Once again, Fuller and Leeman frame my experience in the broader context very clearly:

> "One finding emerging from such research is that the desire to pass on Spanish is not enough on its own. Instead, language socialization through shared activities and sustained interactions in Spanish was important as was participation in language-focused and literacy-related events, whether these were centered on religious activities, schoolwork, movie-watching, or pleasure reading."

In my conversation with Elaine, I learned about a language path that differed from my own and my siblings'. Elaine grew up with only Spanish in the home, but she says her mom always told the story of how confident she was on the first day of school. She was grounded, and she knew she had enough of a foundation in both languages to feel confident. When she began researching the topic of bilingual education, she learned that her experience was not unique. The research showed that children who have a strong foundation in their native language actually experience an easier transition into learning a second language.

This near-total reliance on the home and family for Spanish acquisition has left many people like me behind, falling through the cracks. Similarly, it sets up a dynamic that Mark Hugo López described to me during our conversation about his research for the Pew Research Center. By the third generation, it is less common for there to be any Spanish retention. So even if the efforts of a family unit to maintain Spanish are sufficient for their second-generation children, the outlook is usually not better by the third. Without a broader consensus that bilingualism and true bilingual education should be a priority and offer significant value to our society, the game feels rigged.

In fact, I had the opportunity to speak with a group of third-generation family members as part of this project. My second cousin Chris described his Spanish as somewhere between bare minimum and semi-fluent, noting that what Spanish he does have comes from family members who spoke it in his household growing up and some input from school. My two sons, Rodney Jr. and Roman, and my nephew Joey added to this by explaining how they did take Spanish at school, but it was often patchy and not focused on conversation. Jordan was only very briefly able to study Spanish at school before the school's focus shifted to music, and Spanish was left behind entirely.

None of the third-generation members reported being fluent in Spanish, and it was clear that the efforts at home were not enough to counter the monolingual culture in which they were raised. Interestingly, my nephew Jordan told us that he specifically hired a Spanish-speaking babysitter and asked her to speak to his young daughter in Spanish. "She has a better opportunity than I did," he remarked.

My Shift to Spanish

Posing with Jeff Smith and Pat Romero at my graduation from New York University. Jeff and Pat were incredible mentors and guides for me, particularly on my journey negotiating language and race.

In junior high, I became close to a couple I met through church. Jeff was African American, and Pat was Puerto Rican. They became somewhat of a refuge for me during this period when my parents' relationship had become volatile, and I found my home situation stressful. I found comfort and support with Jeff and Pat, who took me under their wings and served as kind of an aunt and uncle figure for me.

Jeff had been a professional touring musician in his younger years, performing and recording with well-known artists. However, he eventually set music aside when he married and settled into a career as a computer and systems consultant, embracing the responsibilities of adult life. Pat was an artist whose talent for drawing led to a career as a fashion designer and pattern maker, working in the prestigious New York fashion industry for companies like Liz Claiborne. The time I spent in their Parkchester apartment in the Bronx, where I would take the bus from Norwood to spend weekends with them, was inspiring and nurturing. They took a genuine interest in my development at a formative time, offering guidance, support, and stability that my parents, despite their love, were unable to provide at that moment. The family-like relationship I had with this kind couple gave me tools for wholeness I didn't even know I was missing, starting with their insistence that I reclaim the value of Spanish in my education.

While I was busy learning French in the ninth grade, Jeff and Pat began working to convince me that I should do something different. I was proud of my progress with French, and I even felt like I had some kind of special talent for the language. But Jeff and Pat began, gently at first, to push back. They began to question, "What is this Puerto Rican kid from the Bronx going to do with French? How many people are you going to speak French to every day?" I began to agree that it was ridiculous, but I didn't have a choice in the matter at the time.

REPORT TO PARENTS

SCHOOL JHS 80	**LAST NAME** Lopez **FIRST** Rodney **ID NUMBER**
TERM BEGINNING 9/87	**HOMEROOM TEACHER** Mr. Coppedo **GRADE** 9 **HOMEROOM** 310 **CLASS** 9SP1 **BOROUGH** Bronx

SUBJECT	Conduct	1st Quarter Rating	Conduct	Mid-Year Exam	2nd Quarter Rating	Conduct	3rd Quarter Rating	Conduct	Regents (R) or City Wide (CW) R CW Grade	Final Rating
ENGLISH		90			95		95			96
SOCIAL STUDIES		95			98		98			98
MATHEMATICS		93			94		94			93
SCIENCE		92			92		90			95
SECOND LANG (French)		90			90					90
TECHNOLOGY										
HOME & CAREER SKILLS										
ART										
MUSIC		95			98		99			99
HEALTH EDUCATION		S			85		85			85
PHYSICAL EDUCATION										
Typing		96			99					
Computers							90			90

Parent's Signature — First Quarter

Standardized Test Scores	Date	Score	Standardized Test Scores	Date	Score	ATTENDANCE	1st Quarter	2nd Quarter	3rd Quarter	4th Quarter
NYC READING			NYC MATHEMATICS			Days Absent	4	3	0	
PCT READING			RCT MATHEMATICS			Days Late	0	1	0	

My final report card from J.H.S. 80. Not bad, huh? As you can see, my grades in French were high enough to continue, but Jeff and Pat would have none of it.

When I went to high school, Jeff and Pat made it clear they thought I needed to switch from French to Spanish. "You can't be Puerto Rican and not speak any Spanish," was, more or less, what they told me, and they reminded me that French was not relevant to my life in the same way. Still, it was a hard decision, because I wanted to keep working on my academic progress with French, rather than switching and losing a year. Jeff and Pat told me to just give myself a pat on the back for what I had learned in French and move on, because I needed Spanish. Finally, I was going to face the words that had been in the background of my life straight on and try to push past the shame enough to at least learn a little of my language.

CHAPTER SEVEN

FROM JE PARLE FRANÇAIS TO YO HABLO ESPAÑOL

"The limits of my language mean the limits of my world."
—Ludwig Wittgenstein

"By the end of this century, Spanish speakers will comprise the biggest minority group in the U.S., a country where students in high schools and colleges are encouraged to take French classes because French is considered more 'cultured.' But for a language to remain alive it must be used."
—*Borderlands/La Frontera: The New Mestiza,*
by Gloria Anzaldúa

The Triboro Kid: Going to High School in Queens

Who could've imagined that this Puerto Rican kid from the Bronx would have to go to high school in Queens to learn Spanish? Yet, that's how it happened for me.

If it hadn't been for Jeff and Pat, I would have continued with French in high school instead of switching to Spanish. I had earned good grades in the subject, and it felt like wasted effort, but my mentors' intervention helped me see that an education is about a lot more than grades.

And high school was a time for me to build resilience and learn that to be excellent, you have to move in circles with people who are better than you, and that being humbled at times is all part of the process. I left the

Bronx for the first time, having been accepted to Townsend Harris High School in Queens, an honor and a challenge I am grateful for to this day. The dynamics I experienced in high school were, in many ways, the inverse of what I experienced in junior high. In the Bronx, I had been in a Black-and-Brown majority, with many of my fellow students tracing their roots to the Caribbean. In Flushing, Queens, I was one of only a handful of Black or Brown students.

A few of my boys from 9 SP at J.H.S. 80: Luis, Tony, and Nelson. Riding the NYC subway for a class trip in junior high was a treat. Going to high school in Queens, it became part of the daily grind.

While J.H.S. 80 had been a short walk from home in the Bronx, commuting to Queens every day was a big undertaking. Before I attended Townsend Harris, trips out of my borough were a big deal. A bus and subway trip to see a Mets game, a class trip to the theater, or even going to a movie in Manhattan had given me a taste of what it was like to get around New York, a rite of passage for kids in this city for generations. But now I was taking buses and the subway for nearly two hours each way every day to get to school. Leaving my community was a drastic change, bringing with it a sensation of freedom mixed with overwhelm as I took three trains and two buses each day, getting up at 6 a.m. to make the commute work.

Escribo Esta Carta Para Pedir Información

Townsend Harris was much smaller than my junior high, with well under a thousand students total, but it was an elite school, with top students from every borough of the city. We had to take both a foreign language and a classical language, so I chose Latin instead of Greek, thinking it would be easier not to have to learn a whole new alphabet, and Spanish, because Jeff and Pat had convinced me it was time to prioritize my own family language. Since I'd never studied Spanish formally, I started as a sophomore in Spanish Level 1 with Ms. Crozzoli, an Italian woman who was not a native speaker but spoke fluent Spanish. Level 1 was easy for me, and I realized that having Spanish in the background of my life had given me a leg up, although I was soon to be humbled.

Ms. Crozzoli, after only one semester, told me that Spanish 1 was too easy for me, and I needed to move up a level. I never would have thought to ask for that, and I was struggling to keep up with the new pressures of an elite high school and long commute, so I had enjoyed having at least one easier course. I was, however, flattered and did not fight her recommendation to have me switched from Spanish 1 to Spanish 2.

On day one of Spanish 2, I saw how big a leap I had taken the moment the teacher walked into the classroom. Mrs. Walsh spoke Spanish with a fast, near-perfect accent, and she spoke only Spanish from the moment the door closed and class began until the moment we packed up our books and headed to our next block.

Mrs. Joan Walsh was one of my Spanish teachers at Townsend Harris and literally changed my life. I learned more Spanish in a year in her classroom than I had before or since.

Mrs. Walsh was Irish, but she must have lived in Mexico or the Caribbean because she spoke Spanish with a fluid, natural accent. She taught through immersion, writing things on the board and pointing as she spoke, like a conductor leading an orchestra. Spanish 2 humbled me, as I realized I would have to work hard to achieve success, and I could no longer coast on my background familiarity with the language. Mrs. Walsh was a kind but firm teacher who brought many different strategies to additional language learning, and we worked hard, seeing results. By the end of my sophomore year, I felt good. Spanish had gone from something confusing and amorphous to a structured and real skill that I felt I could approach. I wasn't fluent yet, but I had the tools.

With Spanish 3, still under the tutelage of Mrs. Walsh, came new challenges. The Regents exams, New York's standardized testing for high school students to earn their Regents Diploma, put extra pressure on us, and the focus shifted from the basics to more complex things like irregular verbs, complex verb tenses, and the subjunctive. Mrs. Walsh taught us Regents exam test strategies like starting every written letter with "Escribo esta carta para pedir información," a trick that guaranteed at least one correct line. She also introduced us to accentuation, explaining the rules behind accents I'd always thought were random. That's when I learned why my own name, López, carried an accent over the "o." From then on, I started writing it that way. Whereas in French class my name had been changed, in Spanish class I reclaimed it. I became Rodney Eric López, as I learned enough about the language to know why that accent is important.

I worked hard on the challenging concepts we were approaching in Spanish 3, and I began to understand English grammar better through Spanish. Mrs. Walsh would say, "Me Tarzan, you Jane," to remind us that communication mattered more than perfection, but I couldn't bring myself to accept that. I wanted to say things correctly. I enjoyed school and had always pushed myself to work hard, get good grades, and learn as much as I could, but this was something different. I felt strongly that no matter how good I got, not even if I were top of Ms. Walsh's class, it would not be enough.

Staying in the Conversation

Verónica's life experience with language and work as a Spanish teacher inspires an empathetic "pedagogy of play" that is necessary for language acquisition.

In researching this book, I was lucky enough to speak with Verónica Guevara, a Spanish teacher I had the pleasure of working with during a speaking engagement at her former school in Connecticut. Veronica now teaches Spanish at the Madison Country Day School in Wisconsin. She had insightful and inspiring things to say about learning Spanish as an additional language when it is also your heritage language.

Verónica explained the learning process for me, revealing her own ethos and a broader trend toward what I like to think of as a "pedagogy of play." She explained that as adults, we can learn about concepts and grammar, but as children, our entry into language is through culture. The learning process flows naturally from music, dance, cuisine, history, family, and daily life.

Working to bridge these two different learning styles, the more textbook and more experiential, Verónica emphasizes the many different cultures that speak Spanish and the different ways of speaking the language. The goal is proficiency, not just grammar and vocabulary or test scores. Adding to this, Verónica always has her students start the year by sharing their experiences with languages, revealing how many of them have a second language at home or have experienced trips abroad or moments when they felt pushed beyond their linguistic comfort zone.

The paradigm shift Verónica embraces in her work as a teacher is one I have experienced in my own life. In her own words:

> "Language is liberation. When you can speak the languages of your culture, you gain a window—a door—into that culture, a freedom. When you cannot go through that door because you do not speak or understand the language, it becomes limiting. That is something I grew up feeling, and I don't want others to feel that way."

Verónica wasn't always a Spanish teacher. In fact, she didn't grow up speaking Spanish, even though her mom traces her roots to Puerto Rico, and her dad was a second-generation Mexican-American.

Through her own experience learning Spanish at school and during immersion programs in Latin America, Verónica saw how remaining engaged with the language became life changing. When I asked her about setbacks and people making fun of her accent or any mistakes she may have made while learning, Verónica explained that she did face these painful things, but she learned through immersion programs that it is "staying in the conversation that leads to true proficiency, fluency, and confidence. The more you stay engaged, the more your confidence grows, and that's what I try to encourage in my classroom. I tell my students that mistakes are not just expected; they're welcome. Perfectionism only stifles growth, especially in learning a new language."

As babies and young children learning language for the first time, we play and try new things all the time, not afraid of making mistakes. The process should be the same when we are older, but for many of us, it feels too uncomfortable or is met with discouragement. As an educator, Verónica believes it is her role to create a safe space where everyone is supported and knows that mistakes are integral to the learning process.

As I went through my own additional language acquisition process with Spanish, I did not feel the freedom to play and make mistakes that Verónica spoke so beautifully about in our conversation. I believed it was fine for others to sound broken in Spanish, but not for me. That message came from inside myself, but it was reinforced every time I tried to use my new language skills on the block or with my family. When I tried speaking outside class, people said things like, "You sound like a gringo," or "You don't sound Puerto Rican."

That type of response and the weight of the expectation cut deep. Others—let's be honest, the white or Asian kids, for instance—could make mistakes and be applauded for trying, but I was supposed to already know. Even my parents, when they met Mrs. Walsh at my graduation ceremony (where I was ironically awarded the Puerto Rican Educators' Award), were amazed by her perfect accent, partly because it came from a white woman. They loved her for it. I later understood that she was allowed to excel without expectations, while for me, fluency was an unspoken requirement tied to identity.

Despite the discomfort and the deep feeling of unworthiness it sometimes brought, I knew on some level that Spanish class was about more than language. It was about belonging, pride, and a desperate attempt to manage the pressure of proving my authenticity. Even when my accent faltered, I knew this was a turning point in my life.

Latinos and Spanish

Rocking my "Latinos on the Move" T-shirt on a 1999 trip to El Yunque rainforest in Puerto Rico. While the term "Latino" doesn't resonate with everyone, it was an important part of my identity formation during my 20s.

I have since learned something that has been reinforced time and again as I have these conversations with Latinos from every different type of background: It was never just about me, and I was not the only one who felt this pressure to be effortlessly fluent in Spanish, or at least to have an accent like I'd spent every summer in Salinas speaking only Spanish. Except it isn't effortless; it isn't "just in our blood," and I had never spent more than two weeks in PR, visiting very sporadically during my childhood. My Spanish sounded, and still sounds to this day, like it came out of a high school in Queens, because that's exactly where it came from.

When I spoke to Mark Hugo López, he shared a story about some of his early academic work taking off, leading to questions about his identity. Mark's grandparents on both sides migrated to the L.A. area during the Mexican Civil War. Despite being third-generation, Mark was raised to feel a strong sense of pride in his Chicano identity. At Princeton University, he wrote his dissertation on the impact of bilingual education on students' postsecondary achievement. The dissertation began to draw a lot of interest, and Mark was thrown into the spotlight, writing an op-ed on the subject for the Los Angeles Times.

But once the light was shining on him, the questions began. Was he really Chicano or Latino if he didn't speak Spanish? How could he claim to speak for the community or publish this type of work if he wasn't "authentic?"

As we discussed in previous chapters, all sorts of research points to how strongly language and ethnicity are linked for Latinos in the U.S. Yet, left to our own devices in most cases and facing the pressures of assimilation and monolingualism, it is exceedingly rare for immigrants or migrants to retain Spanish fluency past the first or second generation. As we saw play out in my interview with the third generation of my family, by the time it was our grandparents who migrated, we likely only speak a few words of the language, if that.

Mark's career took many turns between that fateful *Los Angeles Times* op-ed and his current role at the Pew Research Center. During the application process, Pew made it clear they wanted him to speak Spanish, and they included a provision that the research center would pay for him to take classes and grant him some leave time for study if he accepted the job. This learning process was a revelation for Mark, as he saw the time and investment pay off and was eventually able to not only give talks and do media in Spanish, but also speak to his mother in the language.

And Mark's work at the Pew Research Center has led to further research, showing how widely his experiences are shared. During my interview with him, he shared that the Census Bureau estimates about 43 to 44 million people in the U.S. speak Spanish at home, most of them Latino. Out of 65 million Latinos, about 41 million say they speak Spanish at home, but that share is declining. A couple of decades ago, over 80% of Latinos spoke Spanish at home, but that has dropped to 73%. The total number of Spanish speakers continued to rise, but Mark's research showed this was due to newcomers, not language maintenance in the second and third generations or beyond. The younger group, especially Latinos born in the U.S., is less likely to speak Spanish at home. Among children under 18, Mark explained that the majority now speak only English.

Despite this, surveys show that 85% of Latinos believe it is important for future generations to speak Spanish, and many parents, even in the third generation, try to teach it at home. Yet, the reality is that younger, U.S.-born Latinos are coming of age in English-only environments, even as there are periodic bursts of enthusiasm about Spanish in popular culture. The result is a tension between aspiration and practice: many want Spanish to thrive and consider it a vibrant part of their Latino identity, yet fewer and fewer are growing up fluent in it.

American culture is very good at disguising a global, systemic problem as an individual one. It's very good at convincing you that you have a personal deficit when, in fact, there's an institutional design deficit.

We are raised, either as immigrants ourselves or as the children of immigrants, to absorb a clear message: speaking anything other than English is bad. It comes through soft cultural cues and hard institutional discrimination, shaping our sense of what is acceptable and what is not. English becomes the measure of worth and belonging. Yet the contradiction is striking. When white families send their children to dual-immersion programs, it is praised as enrichment, a valuable skill that broadens opportunity. But when Latino children do the same, the assumption shifts. "Shouldn't you already know this at home? Why are you here?" The same language carries two entirely different meanings depending on who speaks it.

Is Speaking Spanish an Economic Advantage?

I spent some time reflecting on the statistics Mark shared and his story about becoming fluent in Spanish for his role at the Pew Research Center. In my own career, I have felt that speaking fluent Spanish could have been an asset at different times or even opened me up to career options I never had, but it is unclear how much of an economic advantage it would have given me. While it is clear to me that bilingualism is possible, even later in life, for most people, the investment of time and resources it requires is simply beyond the reach of most Latinos in the U.S., unless they see a clear economic payoff for their efforts or have funding and support.

When I spoke to Mark about this assumption that Spanish brings advantages in the workplace, he shared the surprising results of his research. While there may be individual cases where it helps, Mark's findings show that, overall, there is no consistent payoff. In fact, the languages that conferred an economic benefit were those less commonly spoken in the U.S. but of global importance, such as French, Chinese, Japanese, and German.

And it gets worse. Many Spanish speakers report being expected to perform unpaid labor. Employers often ask them to translate documents or serve as interpreters simply because they know the language, something I have experienced myself, without offering additional pay or time off. The thought is, you should want to do it, even though translators and interpreters are well compensated for their expertise when hired specifically for those tasks.

A childhood friend of mine, Elizabeth Ramirez, told me a story about speaking Spanish in her place of work that shows clearly how the devaluation of Spanish, anti-Latino racism, and white supremacy have made Spanish as much a liability as a potential value add. Elizabeth told me the following story about working at a hospital in Florida:

> When I worked there, the hospital was predominantly white: white nurses, white doctors, white patients. In most hospitals, you see the same pattern. The cleaning crew is usually Latino, and they form a tight-knit community among themselves. They primarily speak Spanish to each other because many of them come into that line of work without strong English skills, and the job does not require much conversation with patients or staff. Their task is to clean, and as long as they do that well, language is not an issue.

At the hospital, the cleaning crew spoke Spanish among themselves, and when we started hiring more Spanish-speaking nurses and secretaries on my unit, we spoke Spanish to each other too. Then one day, the hospital announced a new rule: we were not allowed to speak Spanish to each other anywhere on hospital grounds, at the nurse's station, in the halls, nowhere. The only exception was if we were speaking to a patient who spoke only Spanish.

The reason, they said, was that a white patient who did not understand Spanish had overheard staff speaking in it, whether it was nurses, secretaries, or members of the cleaning crew, I do not remember exactly, and filed a complaint. The patient said they felt left out, confused, and even insulted that people were speaking another language in front of them. That single complaint led to the rule.

It struck me that this was not about Italian or French. It was specifically about Spanish. I do not know if the same thing would have happened if we had been speaking French to each other.

When I spoke to George Gustines, the writer I connected with after reading his work for *The New York Times* detailing his deep sense of shame around his lack of Spanish, he described the flip side of the workplace dynamic. He came face-to-face with the same realization I have had at various stages of my own career: Speaking Spanish may not have been a material benefit, but not speaking it still felt like it was holding him back. While on assignment for the Times to cover the New York Public Library Comic Con, he arranged an interview with the artist whose work was at the heart of the exhibit, and the artist asked if they could do it in Spanish. George translated his questions in advance, but he felt intensely uncomfortable, and he seems to share my sense that we are on the outside looking in far too often in our careers as Latinos in the U.S., without being proficient enough in Spanish.

Not long after I finished my degree and started working in public relations, I was working for the Upper Manhattan Empowerment Zone, the economic development organization I mentioned earlier. I lobbied to have our monthly company newsletter be fully bilingual. When a colleague suggested we save time by running Spanish summaries instead of full articles, I pushed back. I wanted our Spanish-speaking community to have the entire text and their own front page, which meant designing the newsletter so it could be read in its entirety, front to back, in both English and Spanish.

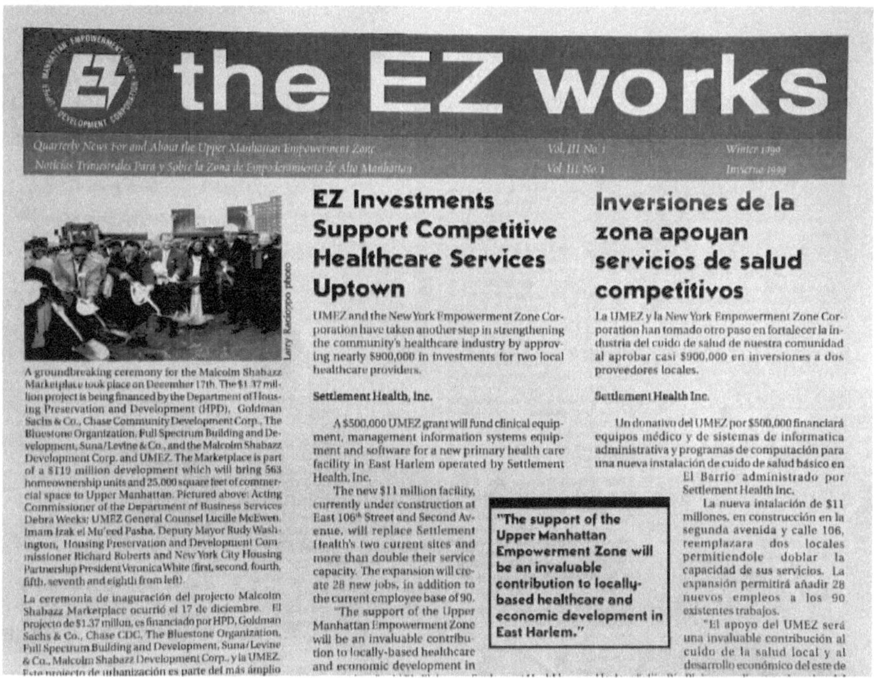

One of my responsibilities at UMEZ was creating our quarterly newsletter. I wanted the Spanish-speaking community to have full article translations and a front-to-back reading experience. It was harder than I thought.

It was noble, and once everyone agreed, I was stuck making it happen. The real challenge came with translation; my Spanish was nowhere near strong enough to translate full articles, so I regularly hired translators, waited for the finished text, and laid it out afterward. That experience gave me a deep respect for translation as a craft and showed me how much audience and regional variation matter. I remember wishing my Spanish were strong enough to get a first draft on paper instead of relying entirely on someone else's work. Doing that work also showed me that Spanish often doesn't garner us a higher wage, but it often means we are called on to do additional labor.

And where does this leave us? Sadly, it leaves us with not only not enough support for language retention but also with very little economic incentive. When dinner needs to be put on the table, it is hard to sustain language acquisition and retention unless it comes with support or some kind of material payoff. Our priorities are often simply elsewhere, even if our hearts are not.

What Speaking *Some* Spanish Means

There is a difference between knowing a language and embodying it. The difference is fluency, authenticity, personality, and connection. Learning Spanish in school gave me greater fluency but not necessarily a Puerto Rican accent. A person's accent is judged as much as their command of the language. It's an underappreciated truth: there's the language itself, and then there's how you sound when you speak it. The same is true in dance; you can know the steps, keep time, and still not look like a dancer who's comfortable in his own skin. There's a difference between moving to the rhythm and moving like someone born into it.

Mrs. Walsh gave me the tools, the verbs, the conjugations, and the written structure, and she herself spoke with a beautifully authentic accent. But a high school classroom is not a place where you can learn to speak like the people on the block or at home in your parents' country. You learn something much more formal. So my Spanish became technical but not embodied. I've often felt that someone who sounds Puerto Rican but speaks imperfect Spanish is seen as more authentic than someone who speaks perfectly but sounds foreign. Our accents carry our identity; they're inseparable from fluency, though we rarely treat them with equal importance.

What I learned in school was Spanish as a second language, not as a heritage one. It was formal, neutralized, detached from culture. I wasn't supported in developing Spanish as a living connection to my family, as a language of belonging.

In *Language City: The Fight to Preserve Endangered Mother Tongues in New York*, Ross Perlin writes, "the imaginative challenge of big differences is quickly replaced with the narcissism of small ones: scrutinizing other people's accents, sociolects, word choice, tone of voice." We know this instinctively from a young age, and we can feel how even the smallest discrepancies in our accents will mark us for exclusion, let alone speaking Spanish *like a gringo*.

This sensation, as Gloria Anzaldúa describes in *Borderlands/La Frontera: The New Mestiza*, is akin to becoming invisible, silent, or erased. The two identities, the two languages, clamor inside Anzaldúa but don't claim her, leaving her feeling as though they cancel each other out, leaving her devoid of any culture or identity. I know this feeling, too:

> "So if you want to really hurt me, talk badly about my language. Ethnic identity is twin skin to linguistic identity—I am my language. Until I can take pride in my language, I cannot take pride in myself. Until I can accept as legitimate Chicano Texas

Spanish, Tex Mex, and all the other languages I speak, I cannot accept the legitimacy of myself. Until I am free to write bilingually and to switch codes without having always to translate, while I still have to speak English or Spanish when I would rather speak Spanglish, and as long as I have to accommodate the English speakers rather than having them accommodate me, my tongue will be illegitimate."

"RODNEY'S BLACK:" SEARCHING FOR MEANING IN THE TANGLED WEB OF LINGUISTIC AND RACIAL IDENTITY

"Afro-Latino is at the personal level a unique and distinctive experience and identity, ranging as it does among and between Latino, Black, and U.S. American dimensions of lived social reality. In their quest for a full and appropriate sense of social identity, Afro-Latinos are thus typically pulled in three directions at once, and share a complex, multi-dimensional optic on contemporary society."

—*Triple-Consciousness? Approaches to Afro-Latino Culture in the United States*, by Juan Flores and Miriam Jiménez Román

"In 2020, there were about six million Afro-Latino adults in the United States, and they made up about two percent of the U.S. adult population and 12% of the adult Latino population. About one in seven Afro-Latinos—or an estimated 800,000 adults—do not identify as Hispanic."

—Ana Gonzalez-Barrera, "About 6 million U.S. adults identify as Afro-Latino," Pew Research Center Report, 2022

As I move through the world, assumptions are constantly made about me based on how I look. These assumptions often come in the form of tidy, neat labels that flatten and reduce who I am. In my interviews and research, exploring the topic of linguistic belonging, the subject of race and phenotype came up again and again. Colorism within the Latino community and our countries of origin, anti-Blackness, and the othering of anyone who does not fit a narrow standard of what is considered a typical Latino in the U.S. were experiences many of us shared. This standard serves to push many of us to the margins, forced to fight for our own sense of belonging as ideas about who is Latino, who speaks Spanish, and who we claim to be play out in even the smallest daily interactions. How I came into my racial consciousness parallels how I came into my linguistic consciousness, and they are fundamentally linked.

Leaving the Bronx every day to attend Townsend Harris High School in Queens meant leaving a place where my identity had felt like a given. In my elementary and junior high schools, most of the kids were Black and Brown, just like most of the families on my block. In this context, surrounded by other Puerto Ricans, African Americans, Dominicans, and a few white kids, I could just be Rodney. At Townsend Harris, a majority-white and Asian school, the reality that I was being labeled and categorized, whether or not I liked it, was soon apparent.

Before the statement my friend Liz Ashbourne made one pivotal day, my memory of the event is soft around the edges, the details lost in routine and normalcy. A group of us was together in the cafeteria, and our conversation must have touched on race, because some everyday circumstance called for the sentence that would change my life forever. Liz, addressing the group and speaking about me in the third person, said:

"Rodney's Black."

Here's the thing: despite being phenotypically clearly a person of African heritage, I had never, not once, in my life considered if I was

Black. Liz's casual statement hit me like a lightning bolt, and I instinctively responded, saying I was Puerto Rican, not Black. It wasn't that I was offended by her assuming I identified as Black; it had just truly never occurred to me, and I was shocked. I didn't have the language for it because I had never had to speak to my identity in that way before.

Being Puerto Rican had always been enough, but at fourteen years old, I was confronted with a question for the first time: Am I Black?

I have never forgotten that moment. In fact, it put me on a path of self-discovery that I am still on today, as I eventually embraced what I now consider my Afro-Latinidad. I am, and have always been, a light-skinned Black man, but racial identity is a more nuanced, complex, and distinct entity in Latin America than it is in the U.S. where the descendants of the Transatlantic Slave Trade were subject to the "one drop rule," Jim Crow, redlining, and other methods of social control that sought to calcify the identity of African Americans and keep them oppressed. While oppression and racism have been equally ever-present for people of African descent in Latin America, including Puerto Rico, identity has been more fluid. For example, in 1795, the Spanish crown issued a decree that allowed mixed individuals who sought to increase their social status to purchase their claim to whiteness through a process called *Gracias al Sacar*.[8]

The Great Puerto Rican Family

Until that pivotal experience in high school, it had been enough for me to identify as Puerto Rican in the Bronx. The mechanism behind this has much to do with Latin American national identity processes and the

---

[8] *Gracias al Sacar* (literally "Thanks for Entitlement") was a legal mechanism instituted by the Spanish Crown in 1795 that allowed colonial subjects of mixed ancestry to obtain official documentation elevating their racial classification. Gracias al Sacar - Wikipedia

foundational story Puerto Ricans were told about who we are: the Great Puerto Rican Family. In his book, *Puerto Rico: A National History*, Jorell Meléndez-Badillo describes the way that this myth came about and how it was used to create a sense of unity, while also perpetuating anti-Blackness and colorism:

> "The idea of the [Puerto Rican] nation reproduced racial democracy myths rooted in the nineteenth century. During that time, intellectuals honed the idea of the 'Great Puerto Rican Family.' Now, the state appropriated the 1930s intellectuals' racial triad. Officially, Puerto Ricans were recognized as the product of racial mixture between Spaniards, Taíno Indians, and Africans. These discourses, however, highlighted the Spanish ancestry while folklorizing Blackness and presenting Taínos as biologically fragile. The racial triad became the emblem of the Instituto de Cultura Puertorriqueña (Institute of Puerto Rican Culture), founded on June 21, 1955."

So while my parents and other Puerto Ricans raised on the archipelago were educated both at home and at school to believe that the warm embrace of the Puerto Rican Family included Blackness and our Indigenous roots, in practice, this was much more nuanced. There is a subtle, and at times overt, emphasis on a movement toward whiteness within the Great Puerto Rican family that simultaneously includes and devalues blackness.

There is no denying Blackness in my family, especially when it comes to my father and grandfather. However, colorism means there are many subtle ways in which it is downplayed, devalued, and dismissed. We rarely spoke about race in my family, and I was not taught to claim or embrace my Blackness growing up. It's fascinating to think that it wasn't until 10th grade that I even asked myself, "I'm Puerto Rican, but am I also Black?" Back then, Black meant only one thing to me: African American.

And, if we are honest about the situation, the goal was to get as far away from Blackness as you could because it had been marginalized and portrayed so negatively. These weren't explicit messages, but it was the air we breathed. I saw my dad make friends with African Americans; it was just part of life. But those messages were still there, unspoken. In some families, they were explicit. People would actually say things like "Black is bad" or *no somos negros, somos indios, somos puertorriqueños.* "We aren't Black; we are Indigenous; we are Puerto Rican." There was a positive pressure to cling to the Indian or Spanish part of yourself, not the African.

Learning My History, Moving Toward Afro-Latinidad

So there I was, a 10th grader, realizing I'm seen as Black, and not knowing what to do with it. After Liz posed the question, I had to start thinking about the answer. This was the beginning of a long process of self-exploration that continued into my college years. The accelerant was Jeff and Pat. These same two people, the aunt and uncle figures who meant so much during that time in my life, who once told me to take Spanish, were now the people I turned to with the confused questions I had about my racial identity.

They met the moment with insight, creating space for me to take a more expansive view of Blackness. Jeff was African American, and Pat was Puerto Rican, making them the perfect people for me to explore the many questions I had. Pat had gone through her own journey, identifying as a Black Puerto Rican because her father was militantly proud of his African roots. Both were dark-skinned and unapologetic about their heritage. They planted the seeds of racial and political consciousness in me.

We used to call our long conversations "the couch talks." I would sit on their couch for hours, discussing music, history, and culture. Pat often talked about the racial conflicts within Puerto Rican culture and what it meant to claim both Blackness and Puerto Rican identity. Their guidance and affirmation shaped my understanding of race throughout high school. By my junior and senior years at Townsend Harris, I began gravitating toward Black History Month activities, wanting to connect more deeply with the African American students at school and with the broader history of Black liberation.

The Black History Month celebration at Townsend Harris was one of my first experiences embracing Black culture through the arts.

During those years, I explored Blackness through culture and the arts. Jeff and Pat took me to see *Do the Right Thing*, which was explosive for me. The film came out in June 1989, right at the end of my sophomore year, and it captured Black life in New York City, hip-hop culture, and racial tension with such intensity that it shifted my perspective. Then came *Malcolm X* in 1992, when I was in college. Between those two

Spike Lee films, race and racial identity became impossible to ignore. They shaped my young adulthood, alongside reading *The Autobiography of Malcolm X*, which deepened everything I had begun to question. By the time I graduated from high school, I was solid in my identity as Black and Puerto Rican.[9]

But Rodney, You're Not Black

By the time I got to New York University, I was already deep into my journey of identifying as a Black Puerto Rican. The term "Afro-Latino" wasn't yet commonly used, but that's what I meant. It was cumbersome at times, though, because when you said "Black Puerto Rican," people often assumed it meant one parent was African American and the other Puerto Rican. It didn't always register that you were acknowledging Blackness within your Puerto Rican identity, meaning I spent a lot of time explaining myself. It's only in America that you're driven to this level of identity schizophrenia, where you need hyphens for your hyphens.

During that time, I had a conversation with my friend, Elizabeth, whom we met in the last chapter and whom I'd known since elementary school. We went to college together at NYU, both from Puerto Rican families in the Bronx, the same skin color, probably the same DNA. During that period, I began bringing up race with everyone because I was questioning everything and eager to share the journey. When I told Elizabeth that I identified as a Black Puerto Rican, she shut me down. She said, "You are *not* Black. We are *not* Black. You're Puerto Rican, and that's its own thing. Black is its own thing." I tried to explain that our ancestry, our genealogy, is African too, that we have African blood and

---

[9] At this time, the term "Afro-Latino" had not yet emerged in common usage, but I quickly embraced it when it came into my life in the 1990s.

a history of slavery, but she insisted that identifying as Black meant claiming something we were not.

It was a privilege to catch up with Elizabeth recently, filling in the gaps of that conversation in college, and touching on how she identifies now. She explained that the prevailing attitude in her home growing up with her grandmother was that Blackness was a negative, something we should be distancing ourselves from. She reminded me that she had actually told me that if I had to say something, I should say I was Brown, rather than Black, reflecting how the Great Puerto Rican Family's funnel toward whiteness showed up in her household, just as it did in the majority of Puerto Rican families at the time.

Complicating her ability to connect with her own Blackness was Elizabeth's lack of connection to her father's side of her family. Her African features came from him, and she grew up with a fair-skinned mother who struggled to help Elizabeth grow up with racial consciousness. "I always knew I looked different from everyone on my mother's side. My mom had light skin and fine hair, and she didn't know what to do with my curly hair. It was always in a tight braid, and my scalp would hurt. I loved my mother's family, but I wanted to see the part of me that was missing," Elizabeth told me.

When she finally met her father and connected with cousins and other family members from her father's side of her lineage, Elizabeth said she "saw where [she] came from." A cousin with the same curl pattern taught her how to care for and style her hair, and Elizabeth has worn it curly ever since.

Today, Elizabeth remains hesitant to call herself a Black Puerto Rican, saying she feels she would need more time to understand this complex, nuanced intersection of identities fully. However, she spoke about the pride her dad's side of the family expresses around being Afro-Latino. Finding that side of herself was deeply meaningful.

Around that same period, during my final months in high school, I also remember hearing an old saying for the first time during a family gathering at our house. My mom, dad, older brother, and a few relatives were there. It was one of those moments that revealed how deeply ideas about race were woven into Puerto Rican culture.

¿Y tu abuela, dónde está?

"And your grandmother, where is she?"

Poet and songwriter Fortunato Vizcarrondo penned the legendary "¿Y Tu Abuela, Dónde Está?"—a creative and powerful interrogation of anti-Blackness in Puerto Rican culture.

It comes from a poem of the same name written by the Puerto Rican poet Fortunato Vizcarrondo. The poem, often set to music, refers to the idea of hiding your Black grandmother when company comes over, so people won't know you have African ancestry. Everyone has a Black grandmother somewhere in the family, but you keep her "in the back," out of sight, while you present your whiteness or Indianness to your friends. So when someone says *y tu abuela, ¿dónde está?* it's really code for "Where's your Blackness?" or "Stop hiding your Blackness."

Between that, my conversation with Elizabeth, and my growing awareness of race, I realized I was only beginning to scratch the surface of understanding what all of this really meant.

Becoming a Dr. Martin Luther King Jr. Scholar

Smiling with the Office for African American and Latino Student Services staff after college graduation. This office was a home away from home during those undergrad years.

Despite the differing opinions within my circle on the topic, I continued to find connection and meaning by embracing and connecting with my Blackness and the Latin American community at NYU. One of the first places I connected with outside my academic circles and major was the Office for African American and Latino Student Services. That became my home base on campus, the place where I found "my people." It offered the kind of programming I wanted access to and a sense of comfort and belonging. For us, it was a lifeline. It was there that I learned about the Dr. Martin Luther King Jr. Scholars Program, which at the time was for Black and Latino students, since the term "students of color" wasn't yet in use.

I was a journalism and communications major, writing for the NYU newspaper, the *Washington Square News*. I also worked with NYU TV to learn broadcast production. Eventually, I hosted my own talk show on WNYU Radio. Whenever I could, I covered stories connected to people and communities of color.

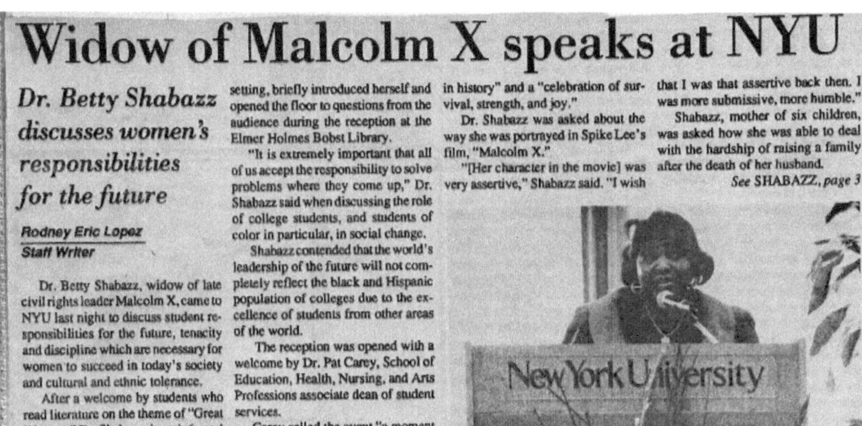

Widow of Malcolm X speaks at NYU

Dr. Betty Shabazz discusses women's responsibilities for the future

Rodney Eric Lopez
Staff Writer

Dr. Betty Shabazz, widow of late civil rights leader Malcolm X, came to NYU last night to discuss student responsibilities for the future, tenacity and discipline which are necessary for women to succeed in today's society and cultural and ethnic tolerance.

After a welcome by students who read literature on the theme of "Great Women," Dr. Shabazz, in an informal setting, briefly introduced herself and opened the floor to questions from the audience during the reception at the Elmer Holmes Bobst Library.

"It is extremely important that all of us accept the responsibility to solve problems where they come up," Dr. Shabazz said when discussing the role of college students, and students of color in particular, in social change.

Shabazz contended that the world's leadership of the future will not completely reflect the black and Hispanic population of colleges due to the excellence of students from other areas of the world.

The reception was opened with a welcome by Dr. Pat Carey, School of Education, Health, Nursing, and Arts Professions associate dean of student services.

Carey called the event "a moment in history" and a "celebration of survival, strength, and joy."

Dr. Shabazz was asked about the way she was portrayed in Spike Lee's film, "Malcolm X."

"[Her character in the movie] was very assertive," Shabazz said. "I wish that I was that assertive back then. I was more submissive, more humble."

Shabazz, mother of six children, was asked how she was able to deal with the hardship of raising a family after the death of her husband.

See SHABAZZ, page 3

As a writer for the *Washington Square News*, I got the chance to conduct some really cool interviews. I was honored to talk with Dr. Betty Shabazz soon after the release of the Spike Lee joint, *Malcolm X*.

One of my biggest moments was interviewing Betty Shabazz. After *Malcolm X* came out, she was everywhere, and when she came to NYU to speak, I jumped at the chance to speak with her one-on-one for a feature story. I also interviewed hip-hop artist Ice-T when he came to campus, and the great Harry Belafonte. Dorothy Cotton, who worked closely with Dr. King during the civil rights movement as part of the Southern Christian Leadership Conference, came to speak at one of our scholars' events. I was asked to escort her from her hotel to campus. It wasn't a long time, but I had a private moment with someone who was a true icon of the movement.

These little moments, some small, some monumental, gave me access to a greater history. Even though it wasn't strictly my history, I felt a deep affinity with it, a sense of belonging to a community that represented the truth of who we are.

Even though I look like a total tourist with a camera slung around my neck, this visit to the holy city of Touba in Senegal was a deeply impactful experience for me as an MLK Scholar.

Another opportunity to grow my consciousness came during two international trips I took as an NYU student. The first was to Senegal, where I felt the profound reality that is standing in the Door of No Return, right in the footsteps of our ancestors who were pushed onto slave ships and brought to the Caribbean, South America, and the continental U.S. On the streets of Senegal, I was introduced to the amazing Salsa band *Africando* and musical traditions that connected deeply to the Salsa I had grown up with and would soon come to take seriously as an increasingly important part of my life.

The second international trip I took was to Argentina, which gave me a new perspective on Latin America and an opportunity to use my textbook Spanish. I remember searching the faces in the crowd in Buenos Aires, desperately scanning for something familiar that was just not there. The Latin American world, I realized, was diverse, broad, and came from many different historical perspectives. Pan-Latino identity made sense only within the U.S.

Triple Consciousness

As my journey to understanding the complex and nuanced space my identity exists in as an Afro-Latino born in New York has developed over the years, I now understand that what I was grappling with during high school and college was something called *triple consciousness,* an extension of the groundbreaking concept of "double consciousness" imagined by the great scholar and writer, W. E. B. Du Bois. The forces of assimilation seek to flatten our identities, pulling us between a Latino pan-ethnicity, Blackness, and our Americanness. Very rarely are we afforded spaces where we can integrate these three pieces and be whole. In *Approaches to Afro-Latino Culture in the United States,* by Juan Flores and Miriam Jiménez Román, this dynamic is discussed as follows:

> "In seeking to find a place in U.S. culture and society, there is at work in the experience of many Afro-Latinos a pull in two directions at once – that of the nationality or Latino pan-ethnicity, and that of blackness and the realities of U.S. African American life. Might we view this, again in reference to DuBois's indelible image, as an experience of 'triple-consciousness', a

multiple striving that compounds and further complicates that of U.S. black folk?"

Challenged Identities

As I spoke with and interviewed a range of people for this book, I was curious to see how often the topic of race came up, which showed that I am not the only one who experiences a tangled, challenging intersection of my racial, linguistic, and ethnic identities. The pressure to present a neatly packaged identity has alienated many of us and often forces us to fracture ourselves to present the facet we are being asked to show in a given circumstance.

My friend from elementary school, Alma McKinley, spoke to me about the experience she had as a white-passing, mixed Puerto Rican kid growing up in the Bronx. We laughed as I remembered thinking Alma was white, until it came up in a conversation when we were in high school. Alma felt Puerto Rican, but because of her limited fluency in Spanish and her lighter complexion, she was rarely perceived as such. Whenever she tried to fit in with groups of Puerto Ricans, she said the "cliques and groups were very protective, and if you didn't speak Spanish, there was really no way to be accepted. Why bother?" This left Alma in a space she described as "shapeshifting," and eventually, she was moved to a whiter neighborhood in high school and subtly encouraged to embrace the white part of herself.

Josue Perea and I spoke at length about his experiences as a first-generation immigrant arriving in New York from Colombia as a kid. A theologian, researcher, and co-founder of the AfroLatine Theology Project, Guesnerth Josue Perea has been an active member of the Afro-Latino community in New York and has worked alongside numerous scholars and activists to increase the awareness and understanding of

Afro-Latinidad locally and globally. As a child, his father was offered a position as a Presbyterian minister in the U.S., ministering to a mostly Spanish-speaking congregation of Puerto Ricans, Dominicans, Cubans, and South Americans.

Josue described his father, saying, "My father was a Black, a very dark-skinned Black man who married a white woman, my mother, in Colombia. But his Blackness was everywhere he went. He was the first Black person to finish law school in the university that he went to. He was the first Black law school teacher's assistant they had in the university. He was the first Black teacher at the school that he taught at. He did a lot of those firsts in these places that he was at, so he was always committed to representing and proud of who he was."

In Colombia, Josue was clear on the fact that he was Black, and he told me a story about being teased and experiencing racism as a young boy and fighting back, even throwing some punches. Arriving in the U.S., the racism didn't stop, but his dad's pride in who they were was a guiding force in his life. When his dad experienced racism, such as taxi drivers refusing to drive him because of the color of his skin, Josue's dad kept his head held high and would never stand for that type of treatment, even if it meant forgoing a fare or two.

Interestingly, as Josue shared stories about his dad encountering anti-Black racism, something very delicate emerged. The racism he was experiencing was often perpetuated by other Latinos and lighter-skinned Afro-Latinos.

"Growing up in New York, if a cab driver, sadly often Dominican, would say something anti-Black to my father in Spanish, thinking my father didn't understand Spanish, my father would make them stop the car, saying, 'You think I don't know what you said? I speak better Spanish than you! We are getting out of this cab!'"

So just as we saw Mark López being perceived as too white to be Chicano, those New York cab drivers thought that Josue's dad was too dark to be Latino. In both cases, language was deeply enmeshed in the formation and perception of identity, as Josue's dad was able to positively assert his right to claim Latinidad. At the same time, Mark spent years unable to hold his own Spanish, leaving him with a chip on his shoulder about how his identity was constantly stripped from him.

Afro-Latinidad: How We Define Ourselves Matters

For me and many others, the emergence of Afro-Latindad, beginning in the 1990s, was liberatory, as it allowed us to fully claim who we are without trying to fit our Blackness into a Latinidad that was often hostile or dismissive of it, or to unintentionally appropriate the experience of African Americans. It also allows us to surface the Black experience in Latin America, something that has not always been easy to do. In her book, *Defectors: The Rise of the Latino Right and What It Means for America,* Paola Ramos writes, "Approximately fifteen times as many Africans were taken to Portuguese and Spanish colonies compared to the number taken to the U.S. That's why today there are about 130 million people of African descent across Latin America, making up a quarter of the total population in the region."

Despite the strong presence of Afro-Latinos across Latin America, colorism has permeated our founding myths and created a process that pushes people away from Blackness towards whiteness. Paola Ramos explains, quoting Leslie B. Rout Jr.:

"There probably are many persons of Afro-Indian blood in Mexico, but because it is better to be Indian than Negroid, the latter is ignored ... The Indian remains the officially recognized sufferer from oppression, and there is no desire to either add another group to this category or delve into the issue of African cultural contributions."

In the U.S., Latino migrants bring these belief systems with them even as they interact with the more rigid racial categories in their new home. Juan Flores and Miriam Jiménez Román write:

"In recent years, greater attention has been paid to the situation of Black Latinos in the United States, where Latinos and African Americans are frequently counter-posed and pitted against one another in a kind of race for demographic supremacy as the 'largest minority'. The groups are presented as adversarial and mutually exclusive: either you are Latino or you are Black. In the face of this widespread and potentially misleading demarcation, Afro-Latinos occupy a crucial place in contemporary racial and ethnic relations in the United States and internationally. They are the group that typically falls between the cracks of prevailing classifications, and yet at the same time stands to serve as the most significant bridge across a growing, and increasingly ominous, social divide."

For many of us, myself included, using the term Afro-Latino to describe ourselves has been liberating, allowing us to feel pride in our triple identity, without erasing our Blackness.

Like all things related to race, the concept of Afro-Latinidad is not without its pitfalls and opportunities for exploitation. A recent pop news story illustrated this, as the African Entertainment Awards USA (AEAUSA) awarded its 2021 "Best Afro-Latino Artist" prize to Colombian reggaeton superstar J. Balvin. While he has made a wildly successful career out of performing music that comes from Caribbean Afro-Latinos, J. Balvin is a phenotypically white man. This highlights how, in some cases, the term can be exploited or even used as a novel means for creating distance between "Latino" and "Black."

(Ironically, while J. Balvin made headlines for these unfortunate reasons, another artist is making major waves in the public consciousness. At the time of this writing, Puerto Rican superstar Bad Bunny just surpassed Taylor Swift in Spotify downloads for 2025 and is gearing up to headline the most-watched television event every year: the Super Bowl. Much is being made of his appearance and his insistence that his performances are conducted in Spanish. Many forget that as a Puerto Rican, Bad Bunny is a United States citizen.)

For some, Afro-Latino has become just a new way of erasing Blackness, another version of calling ourselves Brown instead of Black and aligning ourselves with the movement from Black, to Brown, to white that we see in national identities such as the Great Puerto Rican Family. For others, like myself, it is a label we embrace, putting "Afro" and our Blackness at the forefront of Latino identities that historically always put us dead last or erased us entirely.

The Black Intern

Adding a different perspective is my brother Dennis. Dennis and I are close in age, and despite being half-siblings raised in different households, we became very close in our teens and twenties. My dad had two previous relationships before meeting my mom and welcoming me into our little family of three, so I am actually one of eight siblings: five from his first relationship and two from a second. In my case, my mom was lighter-skinned, while my dad was darker. In Dennis's case, his mom was dark-skinned like our dad, so he is darker-skinned than I am.

My brother Dennis and I posing with Dad at a music event he produced, not long after Dennis' "Black Intern" experience with Howard Stern.

While studying for a career in media, one of the many things we have in common, Dennis got a prestigious internship with *The Howard Stern Show*, which at the time was simulcast on both his national radio program and E! Entertainment Television. While the incoming interns were being introduced to the team, much was made on air about the diversity in this new set. The producer bragged, half-jokingly, about having "the woman intern, the gay intern, and the Black intern." Later that day, Dennis rode the elevator with the self-proclaimed "King of All Media" Howard Stern himself. Curious about who the intern he hadn't met yet was, this "Black guy people kept talking about," Dennis asked Howard who the Black intern was. Howard gave him a bemused look but didn't show his cards until an on-air segment he planned with Dennis later: *Dennis* was the Black intern. Howard invited Dennis to discuss this on air with him, wondering what caused a young man who looked so phenotypically Black to not even consider himself as such.

To this day, Dennis identifies as Puerto Rican. When telling me the story about Howard Stern, he explained that, for him, Puerto Rican includes skin colors and phenotypes like his, and he does not feel the need to modulate it.

Street Race

It was during my conversation with Josue that he introduced me to a thought-provoking concept: street race. This idea goes a long way to explaining Dennis' experience with Howard Stern and my experience with Liz Ashbourne. Social science researchers like Nancy López use this term to describe how others racially categorize individuals in split-second decisions based on an initial impression. This is the race we are assumed to be when someone passes us on the street or sees our name on a resume in the pile of applicants. López describes the importance of considering street race, writing, "This question...challenges the myth of race as biology, genetic ancestry or culture and instead focuses on race as a social relationship of power that is not just about your personal identity."

The Pew Research Center gathered some interesting data from the Latino community on this subject. According to the 2021 report, "Measuring the racial identity of Latinos," survey respondents show a variance in how they believe others perceive their street race based on factors like age, immigration status, and length of time in the U.S.:

> "Fewer than two in ten Latinos (17%) say others would view them as White when walking past them, with those born in the U.S. being more likely to say this (28% of at least third-generation Latinos and 20% of second-generation Latinos) than Latino immigrants (13%). A smaller share (12%) say others view them as belonging to another racial group such as Asian, Black, or Indigenous."

By exploring not just how individuals and groups label themselves but how they are perceived in these everyday interactions where the power to self-identify has not been granted to them, we can reveal truths about inequality and lived experience that focusing only on the identities people claim often obscures. In my case, I learned in high school that I am most often perceived as a Black man if I am passing someone on the street or seated beside them on the subway, and I am likely to be labeled as Latino if someone sees my last name.

While street race reveals another way our identities are reduced to a common denominator, and in many instances, we are stripped of the power to voice who we are for ourselves, it is also an empowering exercise in building solidarity. For me, claiming my identity as a Black Puerto Rican has always been about recognizing how I am perceived and using that to build solidarity with my African American friends, neighbors, and countrymen. While our histories and contexts are different, and I do not claim African American culture, our roots and current experiences are often very similar.

In Latin America and the Latino population in the U.S., having conversations about colorism is vitally important when we talk about race. Why is it that the Black abuela is being hidden in the kitchen in the first place? While there has historically been more fluidity between racial identities and even more intermarriage in Latin America, much earlier than in the U.S., Blackness is still at the bottom of the hierarchy and whiteness, you guessed it, is at the top. For me, claiming my Blackness has always been about resisting the colorism that is intrinsically linked to Puerto Rican identities. When I add "Afro" or "Black," I am intentionally putting that part of myself out there. In fact, putting it first, as a matter of pride in who I am and recognition of how I am perceived.

Today, I have embraced a range of identifiers, each context-dependent. In some scenarios, say a Salsa class I am teaching, it is enough to say I am Puerto Rican. In a Latino crowd, I usually say I am Afro-Puerto Rican or Afro-Latino. Around white people or a more diverse crowd, I might say I am Afro-Latino. When talking to people from Puerto Rico, I usually identify as Nuyorican. The more I learn, the more I am able to hold all of the pieces of myself, because I am all of those things, and present myself to people in a way that empowers me.

Who Gets to Label Us

While the examples I have shared here come from the 1980s and 1990s, and much has changed in our vocabulary and racial discourse since then, I still see many of these issues arising in my own life, in my sons', and in the next generation. The pervasive way that people of color are labeled, simplified, categorized, and reduced is, at the end of the day, a function of what it means to live in a white world. To swim in a sea of whiteness means that whiteness gets to label things, and we have to accept our role as mere recipients of these labels. It doesn't work the other way, because white is seen as the standard, and the world accommodates that worldview and positionality. So Howard Stern calling my brother the "Black intern" or my friend Liz calling me "Black" are just examples of the way this plays out in big and small ways in our daily lives. We are named; we don't get to name ourselves.

In considering Dennis and Elizabeth's perspectives, I respect where they stand, even if I landed somewhere different. I think, at the end of the day, we are using the tools at hand to resist the pressures of racism, colorism, anti-Blackness, and xenophobia, especially in the context of the US. Some of us resist by stubbornly demanding that the full range of possibilities be included in our Colombian, Puerto Rican,

Dominican, or other identities, and for others, we seek precise language to better represent our lived experience.

When we look at all these stories, noticing the patterns and shared experiences, we confront the inadequacy of Latinidad as an identifier and the ways it has been used to reduce and simplify our identities in the service of whiteness and assimilation.

The right to self-identity is at the core of what it means to be a free human being. This struggle for freedom lies at the core of the many choices people of color face every day. We resist being labeled by phenotype or language by claiming our own identities, and each time we freely choose how we identify is an act of reclamation.

CHAPTER NINE

KITCHEN SALSA: COOKING UP DANCE STEPS WITH MY MOM

"This music has been performed in concert halls throughout Latin American and U.S. cities, on college campuses, on the streets of the Bronx and of East L.A., and in clubs in Toronto; it plays in the small living room of a Puerto Rican single woman in southwest Detroit and in the elegant living rooms of upper-class Venezuelans; meanwhile, it subtly serves as background music for a wide array of television commercials in the United States."
—*Listening to Salsa: Gender, Popular Music, and Puerto Rican Cultures*, by Frances Aparicio

The first time I danced Salsa was on a stage.

Well, I did practice before hopping right onto the stage, but the first time I danced Salsa was when I was in high school. I thought since it was my senior year, I needed to do something to represent Puerto Rican culture at the school's International Night celebration. I felt a strong pull to do something that would show what it really meant to be Puerto Rican from the Bronx, beyond the insidious stereotypes I so often experienced outside of my community. It was my job, I believed, to show the other students at Townsend Harris who teased me about where I came from that their definitions couldn't define me. Even a teacher made comments about the Bronx, jokingly saying, "I don't know how you get out of there alive." When I protested that we had a lot to be proud of, listing the Bronx Zoo, the New York Botanical

Garden, and the New York Yankees, this teacher replied, "Exactly! The best parts of the Bronx are surrounded by fences!" I couldn't leave that high school without doing my part to set the record straight.

I had a strong conviction that I needed to dance Salsa on that stage, but I had a lot of work to do to prepare. Growing up, music was always on, and Salsa was around me, but most of my dancing experience came from practicing my moonwalk in the mirror on a lazy Sunday. As a kid growing up with mostly American music, up to that point in my life, I had never seen the need to learn to dance Salsa.

I figured step one would be finding a dance partner, so I asked the only Puerto Rican girl I was friendly enough with at school if she wanted to dance with me, but she said she didn't know how to Salsa, and she thought I was crazy for trying. The same inexplicable conviction that started me on the path kept me going, so I asked my high school girlfriend, Erica, if she wanted to do it. She surprised me by saying yes. She was super shy and reserved, the quintessential bookish introvert, and one of the smartest kids in the school. I was surprised and flattered when she agreed to be my partner for this wild proposition.

Once I had a dance partner, it hit me that I would actually have to follow through and learn the steps. So I asked Mom if she would teach me, and she said yes. To this day, when I teach, I talk about what I call "kitchen Salsa." That's how many of us learned, with our mothers, aunts, or grandmothers teaching us the steps at home, usually in the kitchen or living room. My mother took me by the hands and showed me how to move: one foot back, then the other. "It's one, two, three, one, two, three," she said. Then she showed me how to turn the girl and how to return to the basic step.

Mom didn't talk or explain very much; she demonstrated, and I followed. Those simple lessons, the basic steps, a few flourishes, and some small figures, became my foundation. She taught me what I would later learn were called wrap turns or cuddle turns, where you bring the partner's hand around so she ends up at your side. She also showed me a unique aspect of Salsa among social dances: dancers sometimes separate, dancing side by side or facing one another, before reconnecting and dancing in tandem again.

Mom, striking a pose in the middle of a dance. She was always a natural dancer and my first Salsa teacher.

It was my first time learning Salsa, and it quickly became my first time teaching it, since I had to show Erica what I had learned. I was learning it to perform, not just to dance socially, which foreshadowed the teacher I would become.

I asked my mom what song we should use. The only Salsa songs I knew were "Lluvia" by Eddie Santiago and "Decisiones" by Ruben Blades, but neither was right for a stage performance. My mother suggested a Salsa cover of Billy Joel's "New York State of Mind" by Bobby Rodríguez. It was perfect, sung in English so the audience would understand, and it connected to my love of Billy Joel. Our performance to a Salsa version of "New York State of Mind" was a perfect representation of that moment in my life: a Nuyorican kid presenting his culture through Salsa, itself an art form born in New York.

Even then, I had a sense of performance and presentation. I had already been in high school plays and musicals, so I instinctively thought about stage presence, connection, and how to make the audience feel something. Most people learn kitchen Salsa to dance at parties. My first application was performance.

That early experience planted the seed of my teaching philosophy: fun first, culture second. It's harder to get people to embrace culture until they are having fun. If I can get people laughing, moving, and comfortable, then they will open up to the deeper meaning of the art form. That principle would later shape how I taught dance, and eventually, how I approached identity, belonging, and language.

Once we picked the song, Mom and I rehearsed it until it felt right. I made a bootleg cassette of the track so Erica and I could practice at school. She learned quickly! Her rhythm was good, and we practiced in quiet corners of campus buildings, away from everyone else.

Erica and I, hitting a side-by-side Salsa basic step for International Night. My very first Salsa performance!

International Night came, and it was time to put on a show. I wore my one suit, an olive-green polyester thing with a red-and-green tie. Erica wore a modest red dress that wasn't particularly Salsa-like, but it tied into the association between Salsa and the color red.

We danced our routine to "New York State of Mind." My body felt alive, fluid yet solid and strong, grounded and light. I remember the joy of that moment, the connection with my mother, the pride of representing my culture, and the sweetness of dancing with my girlfriend. Someone took pictures of us dancing and walking offstage, showing my broad smile and animated body language, moving to the beat. In that moment, I felt something I had never experienced so clearly before: every part of my multifaceted identity had a spot on that stage with me.

That performance contained the roots of so much that would follow in my life: the link between art and identity, the beginnings of my teaching, my relationship with the stage, and even the foreshadowing of later experiences, like a moment on *The Maury Povich Show* when they told me I did not look "Salsa enough." Everything was there in that high school "cafetorium," in that polyester suit, dancing to a Salsa version of "New York State of Mind."

Erica and I, executing my first wrap turn. Turn patterns became increasingly complex as my Salsa vocabulary grew.

Salsa History Is Also My History

Salsa means many things to many people. The beauty of the meaning of the word "sauce" is that it can be read in many different ways, all of them applicable: a mixture of stewed ingredients from mambo to Cuban son and Puerto Rican bomba, or a condiment that increases the flavor and spice of a dish. Salsa musicians once called out *echale salsita* or "put a little sauce on it" as a cry for musicians and dancers to put their heart and soul into the performance.

But "Salsa" doesn't actually refer to a musical rhythm in the way we might think, taking the framework as applied to mambo, bomba, reggaeton, or even dembow. The term is less specific in this case, and it is more of a marketing device than anything else. Musicians and dancers resisted the term and the accompanying push to market this dance tradition. To this day, the terms Salsa and mambo are used interchangeably in some circles, and some people continue to prefer mambo over Salsa. Juliet McMains, in *Spinning Mambo Into Salsa: Caribbean Dance in Global Commerce*, writes:

> "Mambo, one of the precursors of what we now know as Salsa, "emerged through the intermingling of ... traditions in New York's dance halls, especially the Palladium, where dancers began with a base of Cuban son, added turns borrowed from [African] American lindy hop, and interspersed these with breaks for solo steps adopted from Cuban rumba, Puerto Rican bomba, and African American jazz."

Isabelle Leymarie, author of *Cuban Fire: The Story of Salsa and Latin Jazz*, describes the many influences in this ascendant art form:

> "The definition of Salsa has generated much debate and, indeed, the sphere of Salsa is rather difficult to circumscribe. Its core is

mainly Cuban and Puerto Rican, though it has included Brazilian strains (Edu Lobo's *Boranda*, recorded by La Sonora Ponceña, Willie Rosario's *Samba con Salsa*, *Birimbau*, recorded by Celia Cruz and Willie Colón), *cumbias* from Colombia, *joropos* from Venezuela, *paseítos* and *tamboritos* from Panama, and even tangos. The early New York Salsa was admittedly derived from son and son montuno, but it had its own *callejero* (street) feel, for Salsa was essentially a product of the barrio ... If the backbone of Salsa is Cuban, its first audiences and performers were mainly Puerto Ricans. And as Salsa gained ground in other Latin American countries, Colombia and Venezuela in particular, it sometimes took on local characteristics, thus broadening its range."

My parents' generation of Caribbean migrants, and those who came before them, arrived in New York and clustered in boroughs and barrios with large African American populations, bringing together African diasporic musical traditions and innovations such as African American jazz, rock, and soul, and Puerto Rican bomba and Cuban son. "This long process of musical and dance transformations and continuities, which had begun in the 1930s, culminated some forty years later, during the 1970s, in the Puerto Rican contribution to the uniquely New York-Caribbean dance phenomenon called Salsa," according to Alma Concepción in *Dance in Puerto Rico: Embodied Meanings*.

The song my mom suggested for that performance says even more than I knew at the time about our history, the history of Salsa, and what it means to be a Nuyorican. It was at the potent intersection of Afro-Caribbean and African American cultures in the Bronx, Harlem, and elsewhere in New York during the 30s and the Great Migration that Salsa was born. While Salsa traces its ancestry to the Caribbean and has had a deep impact on cultures across the Hispanic world, it must be said that it was born in New York City.

Although I did not know this history at the time, the freedom and joy I felt dancing to the Salsa version of "New York State of Mind" in my kitchen with Mom and on the stage in Queens holds deep meaning for me now that I understand why I connected so deeply. As a Black Puerto Rican kid born in New York in the mid-seventies, my very being is mirrored in this art form, which arose as a testament to the complex, layered joy of resistance. Salsa, just like me, is Afro-Caribbean, it's New York, it's the Bronx, and it's most at home when expressing mastery through joy and playful self-expression.

Afro-Latinidad and Salsa

"If New York shaped Puerto Rican-ness, so too did Puerto Ricans shape New York, and the look and sound of black New York in particular. Part of the rationale for and result of the passage of the Jones Act in 1917 was to allow Puerto Ricans to fill out the ranks of U.S. soldiers who fought in World War II. One result of their doing so, and of being placed in mostly black regiments, was that when Harlem's top enlisted bandleader, James Reese Europe, organized his famous 369th Infantry Division Hellfighters Band, an ensemble often credited with bringing jazz to Europe, fully half of his reed section was comprised of Puerto Rican doughboys, trained in the military bands of la isla. When the Hellfighters made their triumphant return to New York in 1919, they led a ragtimey march up Lenox Avenue that's recalled as the start of Harlem's Jazz Age. And from the moment Reese Europe's Puerto Rican

saxophonists swayed through Harlem, there's been no style of black music in New York, from swing to bebop to hip-hop, to whose making Puerto Ricans haven't been central."
—*Island People: The Caribbean and The World*,
by Joshua Jelly-Schapiro

Afro-Latinidad cannot be separated from Salsa. In fact, the term's emergence has an early connection to mambo, one of the primary precursors to Salsa. In *Spinning Mambo Into Salsa*, Juliet McMains explains how the legendary mambo group Machito and His Afro-Cubans embraced that term "a full fifty years before Black Americans embraced the prefix 'African,' which speaks to the degree to which many Latin dance musicians identified with the African roots of their artistic expression."

Both in our Caribbean nations and in the U.S., Caribbean society has been "shaped to a large degree by diverse colonial powers and by the common experience of slavery," writes Alma Concepción. "Caribbean societies have undergone very complex social processes in which many ethnicities in diaspora have come together."

For Puerto Ricans arriving in New York and other large East Coast U.S. cities starting after WWI, their cultural practice of blending elements to retain, create, and resist translated to this new context, and the syncretism only grew, putting us on the trajectory that brought me to that stage in Queens, presenting Salsa as a representative cultural practice.

Salsa: Toward Belonging

"Latino/a identity is based on an 'imagined community that is 'more a political, ethnic, and cultural positioning than a genetic

or racial identity... a political, rather than biological, matrix'
(Costantino and Taylor 2000: 8). Since the umbrella term
Latino/a encompasses so many different cultures from Latin
America, the Caribbean, and the U.S., neither Latino/a identity
nor Salsa dance can be reduced to fixed, homogeneous
characteristics. Similarly, the collective roots of Salsa dance come
from many heterogeneous sources, the result of a complex
history that extends from the colonial encounter to U.S.
migration. The Salsa dancing body 'narrates' this history,
expressing a multifaceted, transcultural Latino/a identity that is
in constant motion."

—*Salsa Dance: Latino/a History in Motion*, by Priscilla Renta

Salsa was as important to choreographer Sita Frederick's identity
development as it was to mine. Here, she and I are social dancing at a Cuban
restaurant in East Harlem.

Performing Salsa for my high school's International Night was a revelation for me, even though it wasn't until a few years later that I began to dance more seriously. That moment marked something that my friend Sita Frederick, a wonderful dancer I would meet about 15 years later in the Salsa performance scene in New York, described experiencing as well when I spoke to her recently. Sita comes from a mixed background and was disconnected from her Dominican heritage for large portions of her childhood, leaving her feeling culturally and ethnically adrift.

It took time and soul-searching for Sita to find and embrace Afro-Latinidad, and Salsa played a vital role in her journey toward wholeness. She was already involved in contemporary dance, and she described her entry to Salsa as something that felt almost inevitable, a sort of homecoming. "As part of my identity formation, it was necessary for me to learn to dance Salsa, because it was the late 90s in New York, and hip-hop and Salsa were everything." The second wave of Salsa was on fire, lighting up clubs, studios, and stages around the world as the dream of diversity that had existed only in the hermetic spaces of dancehalls like the Palladium in the first wave of Salsa was able to explode out into the open in the full flower of the post-civil rights era. Sita described this heady time, saying, "Going out, you would find Salsa bands playing, and there was live music, there were DJs, it was an incredible scene." Afro-Latino New Yorkers like Sita and I soon found that the steps of our path to belonging were also the steps of a dance that was gaining in popularity and visibility.

Dancing Salsa on the World Stage

And Salsa was really having a moment in the 1990s. Competitions, studios, and industries emerged, and a divide grew between "academy Salsa dancers and those who learned at home 'in the kitchen' or in the clubs through the tradition of observation, trial, and error, and informal community guidance," according to McMains. The racial divide between those who learned Latin dancing in ballroom studios and those who learned informally through formative, immersive cultural experiences, according to McMains, was no longer neatly divided along racial and ethnic lines.

Sita, as a second-generation Dominican, and I, as a second-generation stateside Puerto Rican, exemplified this new wave of cultural seekers who found belonging, enjoyment, and careers in studio classrooms alongside diverse groups of Latinos and non-Latinos who were drawn to learning Salsa in this era. This, curiously enough, mirrors the way Spanish showed up in my life, except this time, my teachers were Puerto Rican. Without significant access to immersive experiences, classrooms were the only places I could access my own culture and return to myself, with fluency in the dance tradition I had been born into but had never fully experienced.

Sita described what Salsa meant to her during this period of self-discovery, saying, "The idea that my identity formation was embodied was one of the core things that I found in dance and why I found dance." In building a repertoire of movements, shared with a dance partner, we began to feel whole in our bodies, the many fractured pieces of who we are finally able to come home.

Riding the Wave

"Salsa is the harmonic sum of all Latin culture that meets in New York."
—Willie Colón

As my mom took my hand and led me on my first steps toward a dancer's life, Salsa was experiencing a resurgence and growing in popularity in a way that hindsight shows would result in it exploding onto the world stage, with conferences, popular studios, contests, and a new nightclub scene.

The early generations of Salsa and its predecessors, born in the 30s and shaped by the Great Migration in New York in the 40s, 50s, and 60s, had faded, and Salsa had become little more than nostalgia for those who experienced it firsthand. But in the early 1990s, glimmers of a resurgence emerged, marking what I think of as the first wave of the second Salsa era. Eddie Torres, whose teaching style I would later come to deeply admire, was building a nascent movement, developing and teaching a dance style that would go on to take the world by storm. The importance of Eddie and the other dancers who were blazing a trail in the early 1990s cannot be overstated, and Eddie is considered the catalyst for bringing Salsa dancing back to our communities and building such momentum that it went on to captivate the whole world.

Mambo luminaries Millie Donay and Pedro "Cuban Pete" Aguilar shone brightly during the Palladium era. Although styles have changed, we're indebted to this generation's creative genius.

Although it wasn't until a few years later that I really started dancing, it is interesting to look back and realize that my toddler steps toward the art form mirrored the beginnings of the growing movement itself.

The undisputed King of Mambo Dancing, Eddie Torres. Serving as the bridge from Palladium-era mambo to a more modern expression, Eddie was an exemplar of exceptional dance instruction for me.

My dear friend Addie Diaz-Siverio (whose Addie-Tude Dance Company would later give me an incredible creative outlet, community, and platform for dance) remembers the first wave with infectious energy:

> "As a young adult, I used to go to the Copa and all the clubs and Side Street, especially. That was like the dancer's haven. Actually, the very first time that I went to Side Street, I went to see one of my favorites, Ray de la Paz, who was playing live. I sat down with my girlfriends, and when I looked around, I was, like, flabbergasted with the dancers. There were professional dancers

there that evening. I had never seen people dancing turn patterns and doing open shines. And I was like, 'What is happening? Like, what is this?' I was just blown away. I didn't dare get up that whole night to dance because I was just staring at them, and I was just so impressed."

But get up and dance she did, and this experience marked a turn from the amateur ranks toward the professional scene for Addie. She entered dance contests, was eventually taken on by a mentor, and trained to join a dance company called Dancers Fantasy Stars. In this capacity, she traveled the world competing in competitions and conferences, and danced for several companies before starting her own, seeking a creative space to delve into choreography.

She describes the electric energy of coming up during the resurgence of mambo and Salsa in New York, and, in a recent conversation, said she felt blessed to be there and to have access to this culture at a time when it was experiencing such growth.

From Puerto Rico to New York and Back Again

Do you remember the first story I told you? The one where Dancing Classrooms landed a big Univision interview, but I realized I was in over my head linguistically and had to pass the job off to my colleague, Ivelisse Garcia, who was born and raised in Puerto Rico?

Ivelisse is a lot more than just a fluent Spanish speaker in that story. She was an integral part of Dancing Classrooms for many years and a cherished colleague. When we caught up recently, I asked her about the music and dancing she grew up with in the San Juan area of Puerto Rico. Describing herself as an '80s baby, Ivelisse told me that her older brother introduced her to Salsa and cha-cha, which he called *guajira*, from a young age. She was six years younger than him, but her brother showed her the steps and introduced her to the Fania All-Stars, whose music became the soundtrack of her childhood.

When high school came around, the influence of rock and roll started to show up on the island. Ivelisse and her friends would go to concerts at *El Coliseo,* where rock bands often performed, embracing what it meant to be a *rockero* rather than a *cocolo.* She told me that rock music transcended language, and she remembered singing along to the live music even though she often didn't understand the words. She described how this period felt for her and her peers in Puerto Rico, saying, "I described it as the beginning of America slowly coming into Puerto Rico."

When Ivelisse found her calling, she sought a college dance program to attend. Finding none in Puerto Rico, she ended up in Boston. Curiously enough, Ivelisse was raised in Puerto Rico and introduced to a bit of Salsa early on in her childhood, but it was still in a formal dance class setting where she really began to dance Salsa, just like me and many others in our generation.

Although Ivelisse had taken the requisite English courses throughout her schooling in Puerto Rico, she never had the wraparound support or intensive teaching that we have seen throughout our discussions of Spanish instruction in the U.S., which is needed for a student to acquire an additional language. It wasn't until she arrived in Boston and was thrown into the deep end of immersion that she had enough exposure, opportunities for practice, and a reason for learning to become fluent in written and spoken English. Before her passion and talent for dance brought her to the U.S., Ivelisse said, "There was no reason for us to learn English." It was just another subject at school in Puerto Rico, not an opportunity at bilingualism.

Looking at the history and the stories my friends and colleagues have shared, I see how clearly my journey to dance maps onto the cultural history of Salsa itself. It was no accident that my initiation was on a stage, performing for a majority non-Latino crowd.

CHAPTER TEN

FINDING DANCE. OR DID IT FIND ME?

"When breaking the basic step down, one might mistake it for a simple one, but to be able to dance in rhythm with the music and in synch with a partner, a complex combination of musicality and virtuosity is required, as well as a great deal of versatility."

—*Dance in Puerto Rico: Embodied Meanings*, by Alma Concepción

Seeing the World Through an International Lens

As I walked through the streets of Dakar, my mind raced as my nervous system tried to take everything in. I'd never experienced anything like this, and I soaked up the new sights, smells, sounds, and the sensation of walking through crowd after crowd of Black people with only the occasional white face. The very act of setting foot on African land felt sacred and important.

At nineteen, I had a few years of learning about the African side of my Puerto Rican ancestry, so being on the continent for the first time felt like a chance to gain firsthand experience of African culture. Africa went from an abstraction to a real place, and I saw it with my own eyes rather than through a book, a story, or a media representation. While my identity was still in formation, this trip was an important affirmation of my Afro-Latinidad and my connection to a larger diaspora.

I took this trip to Senegal in 1993, along with a group of fellow Martin Luther King Jr. Scholars from NYU. We were hosted by a group of students from the University of Dakar. As I was immersed in the excitement of this adventure, my ear caught the strains of a familiar sound.

Salsa.

But how? Salsa in Dakar, Senegal? The juxtaposition of something so familiar, this music I had grown up hearing, music that felt like home for me, in such an unfamiliar setting had my full attention. I listened to a group whose song "Yay Boy" would go on to become one of the smash hits of the Salsa resurgence "Africando." I could barely believe my ears. The melodies, rhythms, and instruments sounded so Caribbean, yet the vocalist was singing in Wolof. Hearing organic Salsa in Senegal revealed this powerful circular migration of culture: Africa influencing the Caribbean and New York, and then Salsa returning to West Africa.

* * *

A year had passed since my MLK Scholar colleagues and I were hosted by the University of Dakar, and this time, we were in Buenos Aires, Argentina. This was a profound experience for me, as I was able to use my high school Spanish in an immersive setting for the first time, but equally, I came up against the reality of the diversity in Latin America, experiencing a different Spanish from what my parents spoke, or Mrs. Walsh had taught me four years prior. It was a revelation for me, as a visiting student, to practice my Spanish with a sense of anonymity and distance. I didn't have the pressure to pop out with a perfect, unstudied Puerto Rican accent, as I felt I had to at home in New York. For the first time in my life, I could just be "one of those American students," and the high school Spanish I had was seen as a welcome surprise, not a sign for the door to Latinidad to be slammed in my face.

I have a picture from that trip: I am holding an Argentine tango dancer in my arms, posing as if I know what I am doing, and her leg is curved artfully around me. The picture, a gimmick for tourists that I treasure nonetheless, was from the night I was introduced to tango when we went to a live performance. I had no idea that in a few short years, I would be working alongside some of the best Argentine tango dancers in the world. That night, I was simply stunned by an incredible performance that opened my eyes to the artistry, passion, and potential of social dance.

Posing with a professional tango dancer after a performance when visiting Buenos Aires as an MLK Scholar. In just a few years, I'd be colleagues with some of the best tango artists in the world.

Meeting a Salsera

After my junior year at NYU, in the summer of 1994, I had an internship doing community interviews in the South Bronx. My coworkers, the full-time employees I thought of as the "adults," often invited me to after-work events, and it was with them that I became aware of the rising popularity of Salsa.

At an event I attended with this group of coworkers, Salsa music played, and people danced. I thought it was all pretty cool, even more so when I saw a young woman who was a fantastic Salsa dancer. I was blown away by how she was moving, how confident and skilled she was. At one point, we were standing next to each other, and I introduced myself. She asked me to dance, and I said I didn't know how. She gently insisted I should just try it. I had never felt so intrigued yet clumsy in my life as that first dance with Eleanor.

The next day, I was talking with a coworker named Pedro, one of the senior guys. He was a very cool, handsome Puerto Rican guy. I told him about the event and about my dance with Eleanor. He said, "Oh, that woman, she's a *salsera*!" That was the first time I had heard that term. He said, "That girl's a *salsera*. She was just being nice to you."

Hanging Out with the Dancers

Eleanor and I crossed paths again later that summer at another event. Like me, Eleanor was a Puerto Rican born and raised in the Bronx. She was a community outreach worker, and there was some overlap with the organization she worked for and the one where I was an intern. I was twenty at the time, and I later found out she was twenty-eight. I was smitten.

Being smitten with Eleanor meant being smitten with Salsa as well; it was a package deal. She began inviting me along to events where there was dancing, and I never missed an opportunity to spend some time with her. By the end of the summer, I was spending more time with her and making my way into the Salsa scene as a result.

By the time I returned to classes, Eleanor and I were dating. She introduced me to the world of Salsa nightclubs, which I had never experienced before. A Salsa resurgence was well underway in New York in the mid-

1990s, and the nightlife was electric. The Palladium mambo era of the 1950s and 60s had declined, but pioneers like Eddie Torres, who danced with Tito Puente, brought Salsa dancing back to young people. Clubs were thriving again with both DJs and live bands. Places like the Latin Quarter, Club Broadway, Broadway 2, Bayamo, and, of course, the Copacabana offered venues for Salsa bands to perform.

My first performance as an adult with professional Salsa dancers, Eleanor López and Herminia "Negra" Lugo. Eleanor introduced me to the world of Salsa dance, and I was forever changed.

Walking into a club was magical, if overwhelming for a kid like me who didn't know what I was doing yet. You left the street behind, checked your coat, paid the cover, and stepped into a dark space with flashing lights and tables surrounding the dance floor. People were dancing, the music was usually live, and there was a bar scene. Some people were there to drink, some to meet others, and some were focused on dancing. I have never been a drinker, so my focus from the start was on the music and dancing. The sensory experience was new and mesmerizing for a sheltered twenty-year-old, and I began to understand the rhythms, rituals, and energy of New York City nightlife and the Latin dance scene.

More Than Just a Good Time

"My identity formation was embodied, and dance became one of the core ways I discovered that. Dance gave me a language I didn't have in words, a way to communicate. It was a way to heal my body and work through the ruptures and divisions in my family, all the ways my family was broken. I was trying to find meaning and connection through movement.

Modern dance, with gesture and communication as its main goal, became central to me. The energy, the gesture, the communication were all ways to express something beyond words. Traditional dances, whether folklore, religiously based, or social dance, also carried gesture and meaning. All of that was in there and shaped how I understood myself."
—Sita Frederick

The above quote came from my interview with Sita, a former colleague of mine in the dance world and an incredible dancer and choreographer. It strikes at the heart of what many of us have experienced: alienation, the search for identity, and the realization that dance brings us closer to ourselves than ever before. On the dance floor, we finally felt like the many divided pieces of ourselves fit together into a beautiful whole. So for me, Sita, and so many others, it was never just about a good time.

My colleague from Dancing Classrooms, Ivelisse Garcia, was born and raised in Puerto Rico, where her brother introduced her to Salsa at a young age. Drawn to a career in dance, she came to the U.S. for college and eventually began to adapt to her new home. Adaptation turned to assimilation, and Ivelisse described to me how it hit her after her divorce that she had been "raising kids with an American man in very white neighborhoods." Speaking of this realization, she said, "At some point, I had just lost who I was." And the way back was going to be through dance. Ivelisse started taking Salsa classes and rediscovered her sense of who she was. The living room dances with her brother, the steps something more like cumbia than Salsa, became the catalyst for something deeply meaningful in her life as a migrant in the U.S.

It is no accident that the arts in general and social dance in particular were a conduit for meaning and belonging for me and so many of my colleagues and friends. Especially for those of us with roots in the Caribbean, "…music, dance, and oral poetry have played a central role, particularly in the maintenance and redefinition of identities and in the cohesion and survival of cultural memories," writes Alma Concepción in her essay *Dance in Puerto Rico: Embodied Meanings*. Just as my friends and I found in our own lives, Concepción writes about how Caribbean societies developed complex social processes in the space of cultural interface, responding to colonial oppression and slavery with resistance through culture. We make meaning when we create and embody our culture, and creating personal and social meaning has always been part of our resistance.

The diverse musical history of the Caribbean reflects the polyphony of our heritage, and dance has long been a space where many of us felt that the pieces of our whole could finally come together.

So, You Think YOU Can Dance?

During the first phase of my relationship with Eleanor and my introduction to the New York Salsa resurgence, there was always a Salsa band on Friday or Saturday night, sometimes a merengue band, or one of each. We got to dance to some of the greats from our era and the honored heroes of previous Salsa generations. Victor Manuelle, Marc Anthony, La India, and El Gran Combo were among the performers on the scene. If El Gran Combo or Oscar de León were in town, that was a big deal, because the artists from the previous era were honored and valued for their legacy, something I loved about Salsa culture.

Meanwhile, I had finished my university coursework early, leaving school in December 1994. Salsa was the exciting thing in my life, the sandbox I wanted to play in. Eleanor still had me firmly under her wing, and I was still basking in my exposure to the Salsa scene, but inside, something was shifting. I wanted more.

Early on, I spent a lot of my time at the clubs watching Eleanor, a truly talented *salsera*, moving around dance floors in ways I could only imagine pulling off. Everyone wanted to dance with her, and I was often left at a table with a ginger ale in my hand. I told her this wasn't any fun for me. I said I couldn't dance, and I didn't know what I was doing. I liked the music, and the people were friendly, but I just didn't know how to move. She looked at me and said, "Stop whining and take a dance class." I realized she was right. I was whining. It was a moment of clarity. I decided I would stop complaining and actually learn to dance.

So I started taking dance classes. I took classes with Eddie Torres and others. Eddie stood out immediately. When I saw him teach, without even realizing it, he became my example of what a great teacher could be. His command of language and his ability to explain in words what the body should be doing were exceptional. My career in public relations had already begun, and I never imagined teaching dance myself, but there was something about his charisma and clarity that stayed with me. He was a Puerto Rican from Spanish Harlem, and I understood his energy completely. I saw why everyone wanted to learn from him and why he inspired so many protégés. He was that good.

I started taking dance classes, and even though I loved the teachers, I became discouraged because I wasn't good at it. I was a natural dancer, but the technique was overwhelming. I followed Eleanor to a few classes and tried to stick with it, but eventually I quit. It was frustrating. I told myself I couldn't do it, and that feeling stuck with me. Later, I realized that experience taught me something important: never forget what it feels like to be a beginner. That lesson became a core part of my teaching. Even today, when I teach dance, people appreciate that I meet them where they are because I remember what it felt like to be frustrated and to doubt myself. It's the same mindset I had when I struggled with Spanish, the same internal dialogue of wanting to be good without putting in the hours to achieve mastery.

After a while, I had a small epiphany. I realized I was doing this for Eleanor, not for myself. Once I decided to dance for my own enjoyment, everything shifted. I started going to classes on my own and began having fun. Without Eleanor next to me, I relaxed. I danced with other beginners and finally understood what she meant when she said the dance floor was play. This lesson has reverberated throughout my life and fundamentally changed how I look at learning. Being able to access playful energy allowed me to learn and grow in ways that were blocked when I was tense and entirely results-focused.

When I got out of my head and stopped trying to be perfect, I started to improve. I began to enjoy it for what it was: practice, growth, movement. You have to be bad before you can be good. Once I accepted that, the breakthrough happened. My body loosened up, I started to get good, and Eleanor noticed. Suddenly, we could really dance together. We were speaking the same language.

Wilton Beltre, founder of the Santo Rico Dance Company, performing a cross-body lead at Gozamba '95, a music festival at Riverbank State Park. I wanted to teach like Eddie Torres. I wanted to dance like Wilton.

Eleanor was a member of one of the most prolific dance companies to emerge from the New York scene, called *Santo Rico*. It was founded by a former Eddie Torres dancer named Wilton Beltre. The name "Santo Rico" was a nod to the company's original makeup: all the men were Dominican, from Santo Domingo, and all the women were Puerto Rican. That eventually changed, but it remained the name's origin.

I would often accompany Eleanor to her Santo Rico rehearsals in Washington Heights, and that's where I first saw Wilton. Just like Eddie had given me a kind of template for how to teach, Wilton gave me a template for how to dance. Seeing his stage presence, next-level choreography, and elegant masculinity was a revelation. We all develop our own unique style, but seeing the type of restrained but powerful energy Wilton brought to his movements inspired something in me. We all learn from each other in this way, and I am grateful to have had role models who shaped how I move through the world.

That's part of what I love about social dance and Salsa in particular. It exists fully within its own lineage and honors it. When the music legends from our parents' generation showed up, like El Gran Combo, we didn't dismiss them as old folks from a past generation. No, the whole house lit up. These were legends. Respect for our lineage is part of Salsa culture. It's about knowing where you come from and finding your place within that continuum.

Finding a male role model like Wilton, someone whose movement and energy I admired, helped me grow not only as a dancer and an artist but also as a human being who had experienced a fractured sense of identity. That connection to lineage, to culture, and to our Caribbean roots grounded me. This experience shaped how I saw myself and my place in the dance world.

That's when I began to see why social dance is such a powerful art form. It's improvisational and deeply connected to communication. You can't fake it. In partnered dance, especially Salsa, the leader and follower rely on physical cues, trust, and presence. I learned in a heteronormative structure where men led, and women followed, and while that's evolved today, it shaped my understanding of dance. The leader has to master his own body before he can guide someone else. That's a high level of responsibility. In my teaching, I often tell followers to be patient with their partners because both roles have their own learning curve. It takes time, repetition, and empathy. Every person dances differently, so mastery only comes from countless hours of practice. Eventually, I reached a point where I could walk into any social setting, a nightclub or a Salsa social, and feel confident. I had built the tools from the ground up through play and practice, and that confidence changed everything.

Dance Manhattan

Around 1995, I began accompanying Eleanor to the classes she was teaching at a project called *Sanando* (Healing) Through the Arts. Salsa was becoming increasingly popular, and the classes were growing faster than Eleanor and her colleagues could keep up with. Eventually, the classes got so big that Sanando's director, Gloria Fontañez, suggested splitting them. She said, "Why don't we have Rodney teach the raw beginners?"

I told her I didn't know how to teach, and she said, "You know more than they do. Teach them what you know." That line stuck with me. If she hadn't said it, I might never have started. So we tried it. The group split: Eleanor taught the intermediates, I taught the beginners, and Gloria worked with the advanced dancers. What I discovered very quickly was that I was good at it.

Eleanor also introduced me to Dance Manhattan, one of NY's premier social dance studios, where I would teach for 16 years. Here, I co-taught a Salsa crash course with her and Razz M'Tazz founder, Angel Rodriguez.

After some time teaching at Sanando, I joined Eleanor at the new studio she was teaching at, Dance Manhattan. This marked a new era for me, as I went from teaching raw beginners only to coming into my own and teaching intermediate classes.

My experience teaching at Dance Manhattan became the catalyst for incredible learning and growth. It was a beautiful and formative experience. I began to understand the deeper aspects of what social dance could be and the community-building that it fosters.

Through Teddy Kern, the artistic director at Dance Manhattan, I learned more about what it meant to be a dance teacher. She had a very direct way of speaking and would watch me teach before giving feedback. I recall her saying something like, "You're trying to do too much. You're being too technical. You want them to learn, which is good, but you have to remember most of these people just want to get good enough to impress someone." It was tongue-in-cheek, but she was right. There's a time and place for technical instruction, and it isn't at the beginner level. At the basic level, people need to experience joy, have a good time, and connect with others. They were coming from work or home, stressed and tired, and just wanted to have fun. That was a moment when things clicked for me. It gave me permission to treat dance classes as spaces of joy. Humor mattered, letting people make mistakes mattered. They would get the technique over time. I eventually expanded this mentality of joy-centered learning to other areas of my life.

As artistic director of Dance Manhattan, Teddy Kern took me under her wing as a teacher in a studio setting. I was thrilled to reconnect with her at a social recently.

When they reached advanced classes, they were ready for the finer points. Until then, I wanted people to laugh and enjoy themselves. That's what they would remember, not the details of rhythm or footwork.

Eleanor eventually moved on to a different studio, continuing to teach and dance. As with most young relationships, ours ended around this time, but it left me forever changed. I was a *salsero* now.

Looking back, I can see how my journey from the sidelines to center stage, and then to teaching, fit into the broader context. As Juliet McMains explains in her book, *Spinning Mambo Into Salsa: Caribbean Dance in Global Commerce*, studio Salsa, or the practice of learning and teaching Salsa in a class setting, "creates an environment in which individuals from diverse ethnic, racial, and social groups enter a community in which dance skill becomes more important for determining status and group membership than any aspect of social identity they maintain outside the Salsa scene." It was in this context that I finally began to make sense of who I am.

Dance Manhattan also became the place where I met and started working with Mariana Parma, who became my long-time dance and teaching partner. Mariana's family is from Uruguay, and she was raised in New Jersey. A ball of energy, Mariana is a funny, talented, beautiful soul who I soon learned could dance anything with astounding ease and a natural gift. Mariana is an award-winning, world-renowned tango dancer who has long enjoyed dancing Salsa as a complement to her passion for tango.

Becoming dance partners with somebody who is just so damn good at everything she puts her mind to, and who lights up any space she is in with her infectious energy and unique style, has marked my life in wonderful ways. While her Salsa comes from the New York dance scene, she has a broad background and a unique way of moving that reflects the many influences she draws on and her enthusiasm for the art form.

Mariana Parma's arrival at Dance Manhattan gave me the dance partner I didn't know I needed: creative, playful, and informed by multiple movement styles.

When I was introduced to Mariana through Dance Manhattan, we clicked from the first day we met, and we quickly became good friends. We started dancing together at the studio's open houses, and before long, we became dance partners.

In a recent interview, Mariana said this about her early introduction to dance:

"I remember my mom taking me to my first dance class with children my age. The one thing I remember was that they made us dance to a song about the rubber ducky. I'll never forget it. We were supposed to dance like we were washing ourselves with a rubber ducky, and I thought that was the stupidest dance ever. I was like, where are the drums? Where's the real rhythm? Why am I dancing to 'Rubber Ducky'? I didn't like it. I realized that I didn't want to be formally trained; I just wanted to dance to music that made me feel something. That translated later in life, because at first, it took me a long time to get into a classroom and train technically. I took more to street dancing. I grew up in an area and in a time where it was more about breakdancing, popping and locking, the running man, and Roger Rabbit."

Performance classes were the highlights of my career at Dance Manhattan. I got the chance to choreograph fun pieces of music and help create community with wonderful people of diverse backgrounds.

She described the way our relationship as dance partners came together, saying:

"I met Rodney when I joined Dance Manhattan. They had a guest night, and we were asked to do a choreography together. I didn't realize I had discovered someone as crazy as I was. I would say,

'Oh, you want to do a choreography? We have a week to do it. Let's go and improvise it.' We would put on music, improvise, start counting, and come up with stuff.

I remember that every time we had to do a dance move, we would start from scratch. We would have a week or two to put it together, putting ourselves through such excruciating stress."

In addition to working with talented professionals like Mariana, Dance Manhattan gave me the opportunity to build community through choreography. Student performance classes were the highlights of my year, as I worked with a group of committed adult students from diverse backgrounds over two or three months. I always enjoyed choosing a fun song to interpret and teaching the movements to the group. Those classes served as exceptional bonding experiences for the participants and me. I've been a guest at more than one wedding as a result of those classes!

Although short-lived, the American Institute for Vernacular Jazz Dance was a brilliant project founded by Janice Wilson to bring social dance to the larger community. Here, Janice and I are with the great Savion Glover at a fundraiser for the institute.

I also had the joy of partnering with Dance Manhattan colleagues on novel projects, like the American Institute for Vernacular Jazz Dance (AIVJD). Founded by Lindy Hop expert and former colleague Janice Wilson, the AIVJD aimed to increase the visibility and accessibility of social dances such as swing, Salsa, tap, and more. While the project was short-lived, our work creating dance festivals in the Harlem community was deeply fulfilling.

Dancing Classrooms

It was through this powerful creative partnership that the next, and in many ways most significant, phase of my dance career came about. Mariana heard about an opportunity with an organization called Dancing Classrooms, founded by Pierre Dulaine, the real-life subject of the movie *Take the Lead*. Pierre is a visionary dancer and teacher who created this program to bring social dance to fifth-grade students, initiating them into a world of ballroom dancing that becomes the catalyst for change and growth. On Mariana's recommendation, I met with Pierre, who instantly saw the incredible potential in a young, brown-skinned Nuyorican guy to connect with public school students, and he hired me.

Dancing Classrooms was my creative and professional home for two decades. I started out teaching and eventually took on leadership roles. I was honored to see how social dance connected with the children we taught, many of them with similar backgrounds to my own. Dance, and particularly social dance, has always been expressive of our deepest longing, belonging, and our playful ability to communicate and connect with others. I saw firsthand how exposure to this collaborative art form changed thousands of young lives over the decades.

Eleanor, Eddie, Wilton, Teddy, and Pierre, each in their own way, modeled or taught me the secrets of success in my chosen art form. They may not have all known each other, but for me, they formed a community of support. That kind of community is essential when you're learning something new, whether it's Salsa or Spanish. Both are social by nature. Language is a social medium, and so is dance. Salsa is its own kind of language, a form of social communication that connects people through rhythm, movement, and shared experience.

From PR to PR

During this period of my life, my evenings were consumed by my growing passion for Salsa, even as I worked in public relations during the day. I used to joke that I was like "Salsaman," a version of Superman, tearing off my Clark Kent office attire to head out into the night to teach, learn, and perform Salsa. This paralleled my dad's time as a Salsa percussionist when I was a kid, putting the arts firmly in the category of side hustle or hobby, not career path. But my life had more Salsa in store for me.

My public relations career was on the ascendency, but so was Salsa. I had the opportunity to work in a few different spaces, from public affairs with North General Hospital in Harlem to an economic development initiative like the Upper Manhattan Empowerment Zone, and eventually in corporate communications. A break between jobs allowed me to take what I thought would be just a few months to focus on Salsa. The next thing I knew, it was my full-time career. My dad was concerned, and we had some tense conversations, as his pragmatic, fatherly view and personal experience made him worry that I was throwing away stability for a career in the arts, something he believed (and most parents believe) is not always an easy path.

But I was getting steady work. I felt fortunate as my dance classes filled up in the evenings and I was given more assignments with Dancing

Classrooms, allowing me to make this my career, even supporting my own growing family as my two sons were born during this period in my life. I even produced a Salsa instructional DVD, just as DVDs were becoming obsolete with the rise of YouTube! So much for good timing!

Thanks to the generous support of my good friend Manny Siverio, an excellent filmmaker and Salsa dancer, I was able to create my first (and only) instructional dance DVD.

I see now that what I thought was good luck or fortune was something much deeper. I was stepping into my purpose and releasing my gifts. When you are walking in your calling, things start aligning.

CHAPTER ELEVEN

MAD HOT BALLROOM

"When working in schools, teaching artists are disproportionately impactful for the amount of time we spend with kids—not much time and a whole lot of benefit. (By the way, give us more time, and we can accomplish a whole lot more. And, usually, the most transformative impact is felt by the students who struggle hardest to succeed within standard school practices.) Over and over, we see that when teaching artists activate the artistry of young people, positive outcomes arise. (When anyone activates the artistry of young people, positive outcomes arise—teaching artists just happen to be specialists at it.)"

—*Making Change: Teaching Artists and Their Role in Shaping a Better World*, by Eric Booth

"Cuando yo sea grande, yo deseo ser un profesional, un buen profesional, en baile."

"When I grow up, I want to be a professional, a good professional dancer."

—Former fifth grader Wilson Castillo, now Alejandro Mejía, as quoted in *Mad Hot Ballroom*

Lights, Camera, Action

In 2005, the documentary *Mad Hot Ballroom* came out. It was directed and co-produced by Marilyn Agrelo and written and co-produced by Amy Sewell. It featured Pierre Dulaine's Dancing Classrooms, which had grown from a single residency in 1994 into a robust arts education program serving 6,000 kids across 60 schools in New York City by 2004. At its peak, the New York City program reached over 200 schools and expanded to 20 affiliate sites across the country and internationally.

Just a few of the students from PS 115 in Washington Heights that I had the joy of teaching and coaching. All of our lives were powerfully impacted by the documentary, *Mad Hot Ballroom*.

I was privileged to be a teaching artist with Dancing Classrooms at the time, and one of the schools I worked with, PS 115 in Washington Heights, was prominently featured in the documentary.

Over the years, I have revisited the stunning documentary that Agrelo and Sewell created with our ballroom dance residency that year. Some scenes still stand out, such as the Manhattan semifinals of the Colors of the Rainbow Team Match. We are crowded in a school cafeteria, students and instructors grouped along the walls, forming tableaus in their formal wear. The sense of nervous excitement is palpable in the room as Pierre Dulaine, acting as announcer for this semi-final event, calls for order.

"Can we please start off with our merengue teams?"

Boys lead girls to the center of the studio, and onlookers fall quiet. The dancers look nervous but poised, and the camera focuses on a particular pair, members of the Indigo team from PS 115. Wilson shoots a goofy smile at his teacher, Ms. Reynoso, before snapping back to attention with one arm at his dance partner, Elsamelys Ulerio's waist, and the other lifted in an L-shape, gracefully holding her hand. Wilson is a slender, Afro-Latino boy with brown skin, short curls, and striking green eyes. Elsamelys, a usually quiet kid who comes alive performing, stands erect, her long ponytail swaying behind her. She has light-brown skin and wears a pink-and-white dress beneath her indigo-blue sash.

As the music begins, instrumental only at first, the onlookers go wild. We erupt into cheers and chants. The camera cuts to a shot of me, in my capacity as Wilson's Dancing Classrooms instructor, as I clap and whoop wholeheartedly.

"*Tá haciendo frioooo, yo quiero estar abrazadito junto contigo...*" The music begins in earnest now, and the dancers break into movement, causing even louder cheers to erupt as each team roots for their school's dancers. Once the merengue rhythm takes over, Wilson and Elsamelys' faces relax, and their smiles become warm, genuine, and self-assured as they move across the dance floor.

Becoming a Teaching Artist

Yomaira Reynoso and me at a 20th anniversary screening of *Mad Hot Ballroom*. Now enjoying a well-earned retirement, Yomaira was a dedicated teaching partner at PS 115.

"At PS 115, we met the teacher, Yomaira Reynoso, and also Rodney Lopez, the teaching artist. Yomaira's spunk was unprecedented. She had a bring-it-on attitude every day. Her youthful looks and small stature made her blend right in with her kids, but when she spoke, you knew she was the teacher. Rodney was a gentleman from the start. He exuded a quiet disposition but a strong core. His intimate sense of groove made him likable to everyone. They were a twosome we couldn't help but watch all the time."

—*The Mad Hot Adventures of an Unlikely Documentary Filmmaker*, by Amy Sewell

Joining the team of teaching artists at Dancing Classrooms marked an incredible shift in my career. I loved working as a staff instructor at Dance Manhattan, where everyone had expertise in a genre, and I worked with the best tango dancers, swing dancers, Salsa dancers, and more. It was like attending an elite college and taking a degree in social dancing. I was encouraged to take my colleagues' classes and learn from the highly talented people around me, including guest instructors who came in from all over the world. The time I spent at Dance Manhattan formed me as a teacher and an artist, but the time I spent as a teaching artist working with children formed me as a human being.

Presiding over my last all-staff meeting at Dancing Classrooms in 2019. DC teaching artists are among the most dedicated and effective in the field.

At Dancing Classrooms, I was still privileged to work with amazing talent, but now I wasn't only surrounded by expert dancers; I got to work with people with theater and education backgrounds, and more. Not everyone saw themself as an artist, but everyone's perspective and expertise served our mission. The camaraderie between colleagues was electric, and we spoke a common language, having all been trained by Pierre Dulaine in his Dulaine Method for teaching social dance. There was a sense of solidarity, teamwork, and shared mission as we visited different elementary schools to do the work.

In the classroom, students were taught from a syllabus, but Pierre taught us that the real teaching is you, your soul, your essence, your personality, and your spirit as an educator in the classroom. That's what the kids were picking up on. You're the vessel for the lesson.

Teaching artistry is about showing up as you are, not just your material. I've been privileged to teach in a variety of settings, including for homeschooled students as part of a residency with the Caribbean Museum Center in St. Croix.

As teaching artists, whether or not we have theater experience, we understand that there's always an element of performance. We are storytellers, using drama, body language, voice, and humor to bring our lessons to life. Without that, it doesn't matter how skilled you are in your art form. That's why professionally trained ballroom dancers, though brilliant technically, don't always make the best teaching artists. Often, those with theater backgrounds excel because they understand stagecraft, pacing, timing, and how to engage an audience.

"As we got started with the program and as Kelvin started to interact with Rodney, we started to see a change in him, he became almost like a little gentleman, very polite, really committed to his team, to his dance partner and he has been such a role model for other kids because he has leadership capabilities and kids will follow because they look up to him and they want to be like Kelvin. I think that Kelvin is going to be fine, I think he is going to be a big success, and I attribute a lot of that to the dance program."

—Clarita Zeppie, former principal of PS 115, as quoted in
Mad Hot Ballroom

Pierre Dulaine's life experience directly influenced his desire to create Dancing Classrooms. I'm serving as MC of a Colors of the Rainbow Team Match, where Pierre is about to confer the Challenge Trophy to the winning team.

The founder of Dancing Classrooms, Pierre Dulaine, had a story of his own, one that mirrored some of the young people from the documentary. In a 2019 interview for a retrospective look at Dancing Classrooms, Pierre said, "My childhood had a big impact on what I do now. I was painfully shy as a child. When I came to England from the Middle East at age 13, I spoke with an accent. I had half a tooth, and kids made fun of me, so I didn't smile much. I only had a couple of friends, and one of them suggested I take dance classes. I did, and something

stirred inside me. Suddenly, I was accepted through dance." That early feeling of belonging set Pierre on a path with his American partner, Yvonne Marceau, that led to becoming a four-time world champion and, later, to founding the American Ballroom Theater, bringing ballroom dancing to the stage.

While performing in the Broadway musical *Grand Hotel*, Pierre realized that during his daytime hours, he wanted to give back. Remembering how dance had helped him as a boy, he decided to bring it to children. That idea became Dancing Classrooms, a nonprofit that introduced ballroom dance to New York City public schools in the mid-nineties. His own story of displacement and resilience inspired him to help young people find confidence and connection through movement, and he became someone I deeply admired and learned from.

The Law of 80%

"This boy that I've had my eye on, his name is Wilson. He's developing into a very good dancer. He doesn't know the language (English), but he fits right in because everybody supports him, and I see him in the process of learning the dances; he is also learning the language."

—Yomaira Reynoso, former teacher at PS 115, as quoted in *Mad Hot Ballroom*

Working with students like the group shown in *Mad Hot Ballroom*, I soon learned a guiding principle that became the core of my work as a teaching artist. In his book, *Making Change: Teaching Artists and Their Role in Shaping a Better World*, Eric Booth describes this core ethos succinctly:

"[Teaching artists] live by The Law of 80%—80% of what you teach is who you are. Our greatest impact comes from being our artist-selves in the room with participants, openly seeing, responding, discovering and creating connections with what is happening in real time during a project."

To teach the kids something less exciting, like a foxtrot, I had to hype them up with some fun line dancing or bring the playful, silly side of myself front and center in the classroom. In their book, *Your Brain on Art: How Art Transforms Us*, Susan Magsamen and Ivy Ross describe the impact of dance in the following way:

"Dancing has been shown to improve mood and to help stave off depression by releasing serotonin, while dance increases neural activity between brain hemispheres and helps to develop new neural connections."

When the kids were in a state of relaxed excitement, their ability to pay attention and obtain new skills, sometimes developing entirely new motor skills, increased notably. Each year, we observed how the dance program changed students in big and small ways. In the movie, PS 115 principal Clarita Zeppie shares one of these stories about a student who experienced a noticeable positive change:

"Michelle is a spirited young lady, always getting into trouble. Even her mother didn't know what to do about it. But since she started dancing, Michelle has not been in my office once for behavior problems."
 —Clarita Zeppie, former principal at PS 115, as quoted in
 Mad Hot Ballroom

The positive impact of regular arts practice, particularly one that combines the arts with exercise, has been well documented. Magsamen and Ross describe this effect as "unleash[ing] an innate tool that helps you navigate the peaks and valleys of your inner life. And the best news is that you don't have to be great, or even good, at making art to experience the benefits." Showing up, putting in effort, and seeing improvement in yourself and others is enough.

But the benefits of social dance extend beyond mood and behavior. In fact, childhood dance can have positive effects as far-reaching as stronger spatial cognition, associated with increased skills in math, science, and technology later in life, according to Magsamen and Ross. Children often do not have enough spaces where they can experience safe exploration and expression of feelings and emotions, and dance is a wonderful outlet. The prosocial behavior fostered by dance is noted in children who regularly attend dance groups, as they develop skills like cooperation and overcome anxious or aggressive behaviors, when compared to kids who don't dance.

More Than Just Dance at PS 115

For the kids at PS 115 in Washington Heights, we weren't just bringing in a new art form for them to learn: We were bringing social dance back into the lives of the many Dominican children who attended the school and lived in the neighborhood. While many of them were born in the U.S., social dance is an important part of Latino culture, and teaching them to dance to Afro-Caribbean rhythms helped foster a sense of Dominican pride.

We weren't simply bringing an additional resource to an underserved population: We were bringing something that would allow many of those kids to change how they perceived what it meant to be Dominican.

Wilson, the boy I described earlier, is a wonderful example of this potential. He had arrived in the U.S. fairly recently and was still learning English at the time. An opportunity to excel at something where language was not a limitation, his Dancing Classrooms experience opened him up to his own potential. For them, as students, and me, as their teacher, dance became a language of its own. I taught them in English, with an occasional Spanish word, but we communicated through movement and rhythm.

For me, *Mad Hot Ballroom* became an expression of Dominican pride, a testament to the power of arts education, and a testament to the impact of dance education. That film preserves this message as part of the enduring public record. I'm honored to have been part of that, connecting language, Afro-Latinidad, and diasporic identity among members of a New York Latino community.

Teaching Who You Are, Not Just What You Know

Returning to this idea that 80% of what a teaching artist is teaching is who we are, I reflect on the way that an artist, by definition, brings their whole being to the task of creating art. By sharing this process with our students, we contribute to their intellectual and creative development, sense of belonging, and ability to learn through play. Booth writes, "Our greatest impact comes from being our artist-selves in the room with participants, openly seeing, responding, discovering, and creating connections with what is happening in real time during a project." Just as Pierre connected with our students through his own struggles and challenges as a child and his own journey to confidence through dance, I connected with many of the students and became a role model. As a young Afro-Latino arts educator, I set an example for my students, opening them to their own possibilities.

Whether it's in the Bronx, Washington Heights, or the Virgin Islands, I'm always proud to serve as a model for young people of color in arts education.

The role of a teaching artist is to create a container where students can find joy in their learning and build tolerance for ambiguity. According to Booth, when the observational skills that are foundational to the arts become a habit of mind for students, they become more resilient and capable learners.

So even though having fun is an important part of any learning journey, dance education is not just about doing something because it will make us happier. In her book, *Move: How the New Science of Body Movement Can Set Your Mind Free*, Caroline Williams writes the following:

"This isn't just about dance making you feel happy. It's far more important than that. Dance and other forms of rhythmic movement plug into specific aspects of our biology in ways that help us understand and regulate our emotions, providing a fundamentally human way to connect both with ourselves and with each other."

Reflecting on My Own Experience with Arts Education

I played trumpet from fourth through ninth grade, when this was taken. I was just OK, but a robust arts education gave me years of exposure that deeply enriched my life.

Growing up, I didn't have Dancing Classrooms, but I did have a robust arts education. From fourth through ninth grade, I had five solid years of music education in a band. All through high school, I studied drama and musical theater. I was surrounded by the arts, and I had teachers and experiences that helped me discover who I was. Looking back, I can see how those years shaped me, but at the time, what mattered most was that they gave me a sense of belonging. Kids need to feel that they are a part of something. Some kids find that through sports, others through science or math. For me, it was through the arts. I was one of the "arts kids," part of that after-school group that sang, acted, and performed. It brought me joy, and through that joy, I found my community.

That's why the degradation of arts funding in public education feels so devastating. It's not just about losing access to art classes; it's about stripping away opportunities for kids to find identity and connection. I wasn't a great trumpet player, but I loved taking that trumpet home on weekends to practice, even if my parents hated the noise. For a while, I got to say, "I play trumpet." I got to see myself as a musician, then later as an actor, then as a dancer. That's identity formation in motion. Arts education gives kids permission to see themselves in ways they haven't yet mastered, to be playful, to learn by doing. That's what Dancing Classrooms represents, too. It was never about creating a generation of professional ballroom dancers. It was about giving children the same gift I once had—the chance to discover who they are through creativity, joy, and belonging.

Winning More than a Dance Competition

A jubilant scene erupts after PS 115's Indigo Team wins the Colors of the Rainbow Grand Finals. I was so happy for the PS 115 community!

I remember when PS 115 won the Grand Finals Challenge Trophy (Was that a spoiler? Well, the movie's been out for 20 years, so you should've seen it by now!) It was taller than most of the kids themselves, and I still get emotional when I see how the filmmakers captured sunlight streaming through the windows and onto the children's faces at the Winter Garden in the World Financial Center, where the Grand Finals were held. They are leaping around this trophy, and Kelvin makes a gesture to show it is almost taller than he is, even though he is a head taller than many of the other kids. Leaping and chanting, the kids are ecstatic about their big win. Among the group is Wilson, who was instrumental in the Indigo team winning this trophy, with his Latin motion and perfectly executed Rumba moves. Despite not speaking English, he is right in the middle of the group. The children begin to chant, "We Rock! We Rock!" And I can hear Wilson's voice matching their every word, "We Rock! We Rock!"

A beautiful shot and a perfect and hopeful ending to *Mad Hot Ballroom*.

I've had the joy of seeing a number of the young people from the film over the years. Wilson, who now goes by the name Alejandro, still has the same kind green eyes. While he did not become a professional dancer, he went on to become a Spanish teacher, leaving his own mark as an educator. In fact, he was recently named a Teacher of the Year in New Jersey! I couldn't be any happier for him and the students whose lives he will powerfully impact.

I often get asked: "Whatever happened to the boy with the light eyes?" Alejandro Mejía has become an award-winning Spanish teacher, and I couldn't be happier for him!

I was privileged to move over time from a teaching position with Dancing Classrooms to various leadership roles, including serving as a Senior Teaching Artist, National Program Director, and Executive Director. In that role as National Program Director, I was approached by Univision and recommended Karla Cariño, a Dancing Classrooms student, for *Mira Quién Baila*. That experience, although it brought the stark realization that I still had a growing edge in my ability to speak Spanish, showed me yet again how arts education benefits instructors and students of all ages. There is always more room to grow.

Wilson's trajectory, learning English as he learned ballroom dance, and seeing new potential in himself, has been an inspiration to countless people. When I revisit the *Mad Hot Ballroom* documentary, it strikes me that my students still had more to teach me when it came to positive identity formation, releasing shame, and learning through playfulness, lightheartedness, fun, and the arts. This is especially true when I reflect on how much shame I continued to hold about my lack of proficiency in Spanish. I had yet to apply the principles that an arts education taught me to that part of my life. Wilson's story is a perfect example of that. This boy, who entered the Dancing Classrooms program with very little English, went on to become an award-winning teacher. And our program was certainly not the only factor or the only thing that could have helped him look at himself and see potential, but it is a powerful reminder of what arts education can do. Through play and mastery, we begin to see that the real journey is uncovering who we always were all along.

"I UNDERSTAND EVERYTHING WHEN I'M DANCING"

"Belonging is a practice that requires us to be vulnerable, get uncomfortable, and learn how to be present with people without sacrificing who we are. When we sacrifice who we are, we not only feel separate from others, but we even feel disconnected from ourselves."

—*Atlas of the Heart: Mapping Meaningful Connection and the Language of Human Experience*, by Brené Brown

What's He Saying in That Verse?

At the same time that I was learning to dance, I was also building my collection of Salsa CDs and immersing myself in the world of Salsa music. I was constantly consuming music, listening closely, and often asking myself what the songs were actually saying. Just like when I fell in love with the song "Lluvia" as a kid and asked my mom to translate the lyrics, I wanted to understand what the songs I was dancing to and even creating choreography for were about. As a dance instructor, this took on a new dimension because I needed to ensure the songs I used were appropriate for my students and aligned with my values.

As a vernacular musical tradition, Salsa can portray relationship and gender models that I do not always want to promote in my work. This raised the stakes as I realized I needed to know what the songs were about to decide whether I was cosigning harmful views or messages. In *Listening to Salsa: Gender, Popular Music, and Puerto Rican Cultures,*

Frances Aparicio describes the tension between Salsa's liberatory potential and its misogyny:

> "Certainly, Salsa, by the very racial and class positionings of its composers and interpreters, has historically represented, because of its marginality, a delimited freedom with which to carve a space for social change and cultural resistance. However, as a musical industry dominated by men, Salsa music continues to disseminate lyrics laden with problematic, misogynist, and patriarchal representations of women."

Trying to piece together the lyrics is not easy, and I realized my Spanish wasn't strong enough to translate everything I was hearing. I could understand some things, but not enough to track the full meaning. And Salsa lyrics are not straightforward anyway. There is so much slang, so many regional expressions, and different singers use different vocabularies. Even fluent Spanish speakers might miss things when the slang is from another island or another neighborhood.

Many times, I swallowed my pride and asked friends or colleagues to help me translate songs I wanted to use for a class or choreography. I knew I had to figure out what the text of a song was saying, but I didn't always have the proficiency in Spanish to understand on my own.

I Got a New Addie-Tude

Once I left my career in public relations to dance full-time, I had the opportunity to perform more. One of the groups I worked with was a company founded by a woman I originally met through Santo Rico and who would go on to be a cherished friend to this day: Addie Diaz-Siverio. Her group, the Addie-Tude Dance Company, became a home for creative growth, and her incredible talent as a dancer and choreographer had a profound impact on me.

Addie is known in the Salsa community as a masterful interpreter, a choreographer who tells stories through movement. In one performance she choreographed that I had the pleasure of dancing in, she used a song called "Muñeca" about a beautiful woman or "doll," and she made the creative choice to take the song literally and had us dressed up like stylized dolls. Finding a way to isolate different areas of my body and move as if I were a collection of doll parts while dressed in a Nutcracker costume is something that I will never forget. Addie never shied away from metaphor and novelty, and she took risks with her artistry, pushing us all to learn new skills and try new things. This kind of learning, having fun at the edge of my comfort zone, was potent.

March of the Wooden Salsero. Addie Diaz-Siverio is a dear friend and one of the most talented Salsa choreographers around. She transformed the song "Muñeca" into a classic holiday dance performance.

Addie's unique way of seeing choreography as narrative, storytelling, and a conversation between the song and the dancers is remarkable. Her pieces carry meaning, whether the storytelling is direct or more symbolic. Sometimes her choreography follows the lyrics closely, translating the text into gesture and action. Other times, the song inspires a tone, an energy, or a visual world rather than something literal. She has an instinct for a piece's emotional undercurrent and for how to embody it onstage. That is part of what makes her work stand out.

In a recorded conversation that came out of a recent choreography project Addie and I collaborated on, she described her relationship to Salsa, saying, "I feel blessed for all of it. I love being Puerto Rican. I am glad that I am Puerto Rican and Hispanic. I love the music and I love the dance. I always say that dance changed my life. I am better for it. It has enriched me."

When Art Actually Imitates Life

Addie was always finding fresh inspiration in music. Sometimes she would come into rehearsal with a full choreography already mapped out and simply teach it to us. Other times, she had only an outline or a section, and she would invite the company to help shape the rest. We co-created the dances in those cases, but Addie was always the principal choreographer. In the early 2000s, she found two songs and spliced them into a medley. Both were spoken word performances layered over Salsa music. The first was a tribute to Cachao, the legendary Cuban bassist Israel "Cachao" López, who was one of the creators of the batá rhythm in the 1940s and '50s. The poem was delivered in a deep, gruff voice, and Addie thought it would be perfect for the men to dance to alone.

The second piece was called "I Don't Speak Spanish, But I Understand Everything When I'm Dancing," spoken by a woman. Addie imagined the women dancing that section and then joining together at the end. In rehearsal, she sat us in a circle on the floor, almost like story time, and played the CD she had burned. I loved it immediately. I had never heard spoken word over Salsa before, especially not in English. The second piece struck me deeply. The speaker recounts walking through a city, being spoken to in Spanish, and saying she does not speak the language, yet she understands everything when she is dancing. The poem describes how culture flows through the body, referencing Africa, Cuba, and

New York City, with the drum as the guiding force. Every line felt like it was describing my own experience with dance, becoming the place where identity and culture met inside my body.

An early performance of "I Don't Speak Spanish" at Side Street, a staple of the Bronx Salsa scene.

Addie wanted the choreography to blend Afro-Cuban rumba with New York Salsa. We wore electric gold *guayaberas* and small hats, and we had to strengthen our Rumba technique in addition to our partnerwork. The choreography was a physical interpretation of the poetry rather than traditional partner dancing. It was one of our most emotionally powerful works, though I see now that the deepest impact was the one it had on me.

"I don't speak Spanish, but I understand everything when I'm dancing." That line rang out like a gong, guiding me on my path toward wholeness. It acted like a clue in my convoluted identity-formation process, as I began to realize that feeling a solid sense of identity as a Puerto Rican, feeling whole, was the point. It didn't matter if I got that through linguistic belonging or another means. Dance is, after all, a language of its own, and I understood everything *about myself* when I was dancing.

Salsa congresses are a network of international venues and marketplaces for the art form. Addie arranged for us to perform "I Don't Speak Spanish" at this congress in the Dominican Republic in 2002.

The song, performance, and meaning behind the spoken-word poem returned to my life in 2022, bringing with it a consolidated sense of meaning-making around dance, identity, and language. I was invited to give a talk at the 2022 National Association of Independent Schools People of Color Conference, and I created a presentation called "Salsa: Community Building Through Vernacular Dance." Seeing the attendance and responses, I realized people were eager for content on belonging and the arts, and Salsa in particular. I tried to build on that with a presentation I called "I Don't Speak Spanish, But I Understand Everything When I'm Dancing," based on the song and performance, sharing how one line had helped me find deep meaning in my own life. But this presentation was rejected.

I had a blast delivering a Salsa-based presentation to educators at the 2022 NAIS People of Color Conference in San Antonio. Educators do hard work in schools and need not only new tools in the classroom, but moments of joy and connection.

The following year, I was hired by The John Hancock Company in Boston as part of their Latinx Heritage Month celebration. The representative who reached out to me to arrange the booking, Mary Desir, bet on me and the "I Don't Speak Spanish" presentation, which she had seen in my proposal. The feedback was immediate and emotional, not only from Spanish speakers, but also from Haitian Creole and Chinese speakers. It was significant because it showed that this material resonated beyond traditional arts and educational spaces, proving that Salsa and cultural storytelling could connect with people from diverse backgrounds. I saw that I truly was not alone in struggling to release shame and connect culturally beyond language, and I know that you are not alone either.

Salsa: Community Building through Vernacular Dance and Culture

Rodney Eri

I've enjoyed converting my experience with Salsa into speaking and professional development engagements. Salsa has a lot to teach us.

A Different Kind of Fluency

Social dance, and Salsa in particular, had quietly, over the years, given me the opportunities I needed to feel *fluent* as a Puerto Rican man. From growing up feeling like there was always an unspoken asterisk after Puerto Rican—Puerto Rican, but he *doesn't speak Spanish*—I had created a space where I could let go, have fun, and experience a sense of mastery that grounded me in my own Afro-Latinidad. The arts, generally, are a powerful vehicle for belonging, but I must admit there is something special about social dance. I have seen it with my students, and I have lived it myself. Not only did I feel a deeper sense of pride in my Afro-Caribbean roots and even in my place as a Nuyorican, through a culturally relevant lineage, but I was also engaging in an art form that is a conversation between dance partners. No one possesses an identity in solitude, and I was honored to experience belonging with the many students, dance partners, and incredible professionals like Addie with whom I was in conversation along the way.

Caroline Williams describes the power of dance to create a sense of community and belonging in *Move: How the New Science of Body Movement Can Set Your Mind Free*. She writes, "When we move as one, our brains start to lose the distinction between 'us' and 'them,'" and I know exactly the feeling she is describing. Williams goes on to explain that dancing with someone is such a rich sensory experience that it consumes our brainpower, leaving no room for worry or stress.

Partner dancing is also incredibly fun. It is a joyful, exuberant experience described by writers such as Anita Amirrezvani in her essay "The More You Shake, the Better You Feel" as a form of resistance to the pressures of capitalism. I would take this even a step further and add that dance is a form of resistance against white supremacy, against forces of assimilation that seek to flatten our identities, and against the alienation from ourselves that results from factors beyond our control.

The joyful exuberance and playful energy of partner dance is the point. The ability to let go, release stress, and be playful allows us to expand our learning and become more authentically alive.

Learning through Play: Not Just for Kids

"Knowledge is more than just cognitive intelligence. The best learning is a knowing that cultivates wise discernment and

understanding, and that evolves and grows over a lifetime. We are driven to learn. We long to fit the puzzle pieces together, to solve the mystery, to figure things out. We are a curious and questioning species by nature. Our desire to learn is innate, and if we're lucky, we won't have it tamped out of us. The best kind of learning sparks curiosity and, in return, endless discovery; it's your own renewable energy source."
>   —*Your Brain on Art: How the Arts Transform Us,*
>   by Susan Magsamen and Ivy Ross

While studying Spanish in high school, it was clear to me that I would never be a native speaker. But, somewhere along the way, I realized I could become a "native Salsa dancer." In recent years, studies like the 2018 Boston College study of 700,000 participants on language acquisition and age have begun to unravel the long-held assumption that, at some point in early childhood, the window for native language proficiency closes. In fact, the study pointed to the possibility of native language acquisition right up to the cusp of adulthood, and potentially beyond. Possible or not, it was clear to me that I would never have the significant exposure, education, and impetus to achieve complete fluency in Spanish.

But I did get that with dance. I spent more than the requisite ten thousand hours in studios, practicing with partners, and performing to become fluent in Salsa. I had longed to feel this way about my mother tongue, but it was with dance that I was able to relax, be playful, learn, and grow into mastery. I now see that was enough.

It wasn't just a sense of play and relaxation that got me to mastery in dance. I had to endure discomfort and make mistakes without taking each one as a blow to my identity. Unlike with Spanish, I was not teased or made to feel disconnected when I messed up a turn or moved off-beat. A willingness to make mistakes is a fundamental part of learning, as Adam Grant writes in *Hidden Potential: The Science of Achieving Greater Things*:

> "Becoming a creature of discomfort can unlock hidden potential in many different types of learning. Summoning the nerve to face discomfort is a character skill - an especially important form of determination. It takes three kinds of courage: to abandon your tried-and-true methods, to put yourself in the ring before you feel ready, and *to make more mistakes than others make attempts* [italics mine]. The best way to accelerate growth is to embrace, seek, and amplify discomfort."

Releasing Shame and Embracing Identity

Experiencing fluency and belonging in Salsa helped me reclaim my narrative around the role of Spanish in my life. It was a gradual process, from beginning to learn in high school to realizing I would never be seen as fluent enough by other Latinos and feeling acute shame in moments when I really could not keep up, like the Univision interview. Through dance, I slowly shed the shame, realizing that I did not need permission from anyone to be Afro-Latino.

Through Salsa, I discovered the truth that my identity was always mine to explore, reclaim, and define for myself.

Shame around my identity and my sense of disconnect due to my lack of Spanish was a big factor in my life for many years, and it had an uncanny way of popping up during pivotal moments like education, early career, and early parenthood, there to remind me that I was on shaky ground. And it makes sense that the shame made me feel unstable. In her book, *Atlas of the Heart: Mapping Meaningful Connection and the Language of Human Experience*, Brené Brown explains, "Shame is the fear of disconnection—it's the fear that something we've done or failed to do, an ideal that we've not lived up to, or a goal that we've not accomplished makes us unworthy of connection."

For most of my life, I carried this secret, or not-so-secret, fear that I could never connect deeply with others because I was a fraud. And life had many ways of reinforcing this fear, from the feeling of not understanding what people around me were saying, to being mocked for making mistakes, and struggling to express myself and connect.

I'm not a skilled bomba dancer, but like my experience with Spanish, the only way I'll get better is through practice—and letting go of my attachment to looking good.

It was dance that gave me a different template and showed me that I have what it takes to show up, learn, and connect. Letting go of shame has been a decades-long journey, and I don't think the work will ever be completely done, but I want you to know that it is possible to let this shame go if you're carrying it. Set down your burden; it was never yours to carry in the first place. We all carry personal shame, and that is our baggage to deal with, but it is not born solely of our own choices or those of our immediate families. These feelings arise in the context of larger institutional pressures and societal directives around assimilation, racial and ethnic discrimination. Remember, it is not just you; it is not just me.

* * *

Woman: "Hola, fellas! ¿Cómo está?"

Men: [speaking indistinguishably in Spanish in the background]

Woman: "Umm, umm, well, wait a minute! Whoa, whoa, whoa, wait a minute, fellas! I don't speak Spanish!"

Man: "No me diga!"

Woman: "But I understand everything when I'm dancing..."

Man: "Ay, bendito!"

The sign language of the body speaks.
Conga magic, Rumba inteligencia.
And tongues are tied by trails of ocean waters.

From Africa!
To Cuba!
To New. York. City.

Free rhythms and slave rhythms, and slave driving rhythms
Intuitive like roots, rush into this cave in the hearts and light the way brightly.
Like a filament and I see the window open in me.

Bands of light music, sweet ancestral hypnotic calling, spirit rising.
Baptize the moon as I hit the dance floor like bullets!

It was the drum that called me

Conversations and heartbeats flowering melodies into heat of wood and
skin.

Beware of those who do not dance!
Too much in the head to be moved by light.
Beware when there is no music!

No beat. Tone consciousness, moving heart, moving feet!
Beware the knife at your throat doesn't silence your screams.

Your fullest expressions.
Beware when you. Do not. Dance!
COME ON, FEET!

We must dance on every occasion!
We must step into sacred tide.
And imitate God!

"Mambo, mambo, mambo, mambo, mambo!"

[laughs]
I don't speak Spanish!!
But I understand everything when I'm dancing!

Excerpted from "I Don't Speak Spanish, But I Understand Everything
When I'm Dancing" by Bobby Matos and Johnny Santos, Spoken Word
Performance by Denise Cook

CHAPTER THIRTEEN

WHAT DO YOU DANCE ON?

"Within the scheme of inequality, Latino/a cultural affirmation vis-à-vis Salsa dance possesses a kind of counterhegemonic potential that involves the body and accompanies the same, often-stated potential in the music."
—*Salsa Dance: Latino/a History in Motion*, by Priscilla Renta

The Play's the Thing: Redefining Language Through Salsa Musical Theater

While I was still dancing with Addie-Tude, I joined another dance company that would take my skills and perspective to the next level. The founder, Sita Frederick, a Dominican-American woman trained in modern and contemporary dance, whom you met earlier as one of my interview subjects, was exploring the intersection of Afro-Caribbean and contemporary dance in incredible ways. Her choreography centered on storytelling, movement as commentary, and the thoughtful weaving of traditions, showcasing the very syncretism and cultural adaptability that have always been at the core of what it means to be Afro-Caribbean.

Through a mutual friend, Leticia Peguero, I became involved in a project Sita was developing called "What Do You Dance On?" The concept was deceptively simple: different people dance Salsa differently. Cubans dance one way, Puerto Ricans another, New Yorkers yet another. Some dancers emphasize the first beat with their step, known as "dancing (or breaking) on one," while others emphasize the second beat, "dancing (or breaking) on two." The term "break" in Salsa refers to the moment in your basic step where you change direction. It might sound minor, but it's a fundamental difference in how the body feels the music.

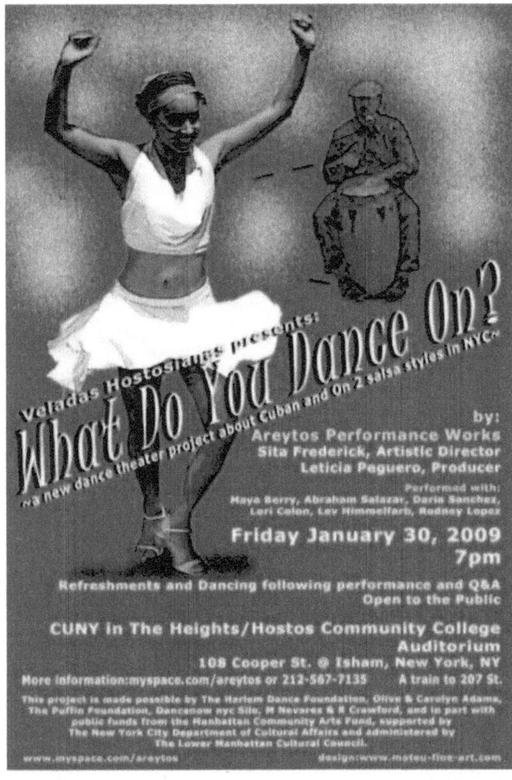

Promotional poster for an early iteration of *What Do You Dance On?* The question is asked by Salsa dancers all over the world as a way to gauge if two dancers are "speaking the same language."

I remember learning about it for the first time. If your left foot breaks forward or changes direction on beat one, you're dancing on one. If you break forward or change direction on beat two, you're dancing on two. The steps are often the same, but the feeling and the rhythm of the movements are completely different. In New York, Eddie Torres popularized dancing on two, turning it into a hallmark of the city's Salsa style. Dancing on one is more intuitive, as it's the downbeat, the natural emphasis for most music. Dancing on two is more of a choice and generally requires training, attention, and a finely tuned ear.

Dance is a language. I mean this in a literal, rather than metaphorical, sense. When we dance with a partner, we communicate through a set of movements, tone, social expectations, and even accents and regionalisms. Dancing "on one" or dancing "on two" functions like an accent or a regional dialect, even making it hard for two people to understand each other on the dance floor if they do not speak the same dialect.

At socials, dancers often have to figure out how to sync with each other before they even start moving. Asking someone, "What do you dance on?" is a kind of pre-screening to make sure that the conversation will flow on the dance floor.

Adding to the "on one" or "on two" dynamic, you have the circular basic step. The circular basic, like the "kitchen Salsa" my mother taught me, is fluid and rotational, moving in a gentle clockwise motion. Most Cuban dancers use this. The slot basic, on the other hand, is linear, moving forward and back. It allows for tricks, dips, and flashy variations. This is what most New York on-two dancers use. So even if two dancers are technically dancing on the same beat, the shape of their movement can look entirely different.

Creatively reimagining the Jets vs. Sharks motif of West Side Story, Sita staged conflict on a dance floor between NY-style "on-two" dancers and Cuban-style "on-one" dancers.

Sita brilliantly took these differences and dramatized them on stage through her innovative choreography and storytelling. "What Do You Dance On?" was a West Side Story-style performance: Cuban on-one dancers on one side, New York on-two dancers on the other. There was conflict, playful competition, and a love story bridging the two worlds. I came in as an associate choreographer for the on-two dancers, helping to stage and teach the technique, and we even brought Mariana into the project.

The performance itself became a space for collaboration and learning. Cuban dancers taught me Rueda, I taught them on-two techniques, and the audience got to see these styles interact in real time. Eventually, the piece was integrated into a larger show, *Bembé, Salón y Calle*, which included contemporary pieces and, occasionally, live music. Performing with live musicians added an extra layer of richness and spontaneity. The gorgeous piece became a dynamic conversation between Afro-Caribbeans and the diaspora in New York, as we paid homage to our lineage, our differences, and our shared roots.

Hitting a fierce pose with my WDYDO dance partner, Leticia Peguero. Leticia is a phenomenal dancer and a powerful social justice warrior.

Looking back on Dance Manhattan, Addie-Tude, and "What Do You Dance On?", these experiences weren't just about learning steps. I was being given the opportunity to play, express myself, and become truly fluent in the language of

Salsa. Each opportunity was a sandbox in which to experiment, to fail, to teach, and to learn. It was in this process of sharing and collaborating that I became more fully myself. Through this culturally relevant dance, I cultivated identity, connection, and craft. These stages of my journey were building blocks that shaped who I am today, both as a dancer and as a person.

Becoming Fluent

For most of my life, I thought I would never be fluent enough or never have the right accent to be considered Puerto Rican. I felt disconnected and alienated from my own community, while I was still experiencing rejection by the dominant culture. It felt like falling between the cracks; *ni de aqui, ni de alla* ("not from here, nor from there"). But when I was co-choreographing "What Do You Dance On?" with Sita, I was approaching a new way of being fluent. Maybe, just maybe, I could let go of my need to be a perfect Spanish speaker to feel whole.

The idea that our identity as Latinos is fundamentally connected to Spanish, for good or for bad, is not new, and it isn't just something you or I have felt. As we established in Chapter 3, this topic has been studied, and researchers like Pilar Garces-Conejos Blitvich back up what many of us know all too well from personal experience. A double bind presents monolingualism and English as the only path to the mainstream, exerting pressure on us to conform and assimilate, but, at the same time, the Latino in-group demands Spanish for inclusion. Garces-Conejos describes this dynamic as a significant source of "social and personal conflict."

This burden is what I began to release as I became fluent in dance. And it is not an accident that I would feel the liberation from shame and disconnect through an expressive art practice. Salsa is culturally relevant for me, and it is an opportunity to reconnect with the playful mindset I needed to learn and grow.

From the outside, those steps may have all looked the same, in the same way a language learner often struggles to even sort out where one word begins and the other ends. We hear the cadence and syllables, and we see the Latin motion, twists, and turns, but we can't hear individual words or see the dancers moving on-one or on-two. But with Salsa, I could see it. Not only that, but I could also embody it and even teach it. I was fluent.

In Conversation on the Dance Floor

Members of "Team Cuban Salsa," Dr. Maya Berry and Sita Frederick. WDYDO was a creative exploration of the various ways a community can divide or collaborate based on the language of dance.

In our recent interview, I asked Sita what the "What Do You Dance On?" performance meant to her and where the idea sprang from. She described how, as a mixed Dominican-Canadian woman, she felt disconnected from her roots, and Salsa was almost a necessity for her as a stage in discovering who she was. The idea for the performance came from observing the different styles of dancers, from those who learned with their aunts and mothers in the kitchen to those who trained in studios in New York, clashing over these important stylistic differences. She envisioned the performance as almost a congress or a conference, bringing together the different voices.

"When I started the project, they would have these big arguments about where the beat was and where you 'break' on, and some of us were contemporary dancers; we were learning too.

We called the project El Congreso, or 'The Congress, because rehearsals always turned into debates. 'No, it's on two!' 'No, it's on three!' It was really funny. Then I would go to the club and step onto the dance floor, and people would ask, 'Do you dance on one or two?' I would just think, 'I don't know, I just dance.'

But once I started rehearsals, I began to understand what they meant. I realized that New York-style mambo was danced on two, and it had this specific feeling and timing. It was fascinating to me.

Especially with DJs, I paid close attention. With live music, it tended to lean more toward Cuban style, though there were Puerto Rican bands and other influences as well. Over time, these experiences really started shaping my understanding of Salsa in a deeper, more technical way."

Addie, director of the Addie-Tude Dance Company, had a similar story about realizing the on-one or on-two difference was a challenge but also an opportunity early in her career.

"Adriana Correa from San Francisco called and said she would like me to teach a workshop there. She was trying to make people aware of the "on-two" timing in California. She had a small community and wanted to spread the word about dancing on two. It was exciting. It was my first gig or workshop on my own, using my own name. I went, and it was amazing. The workshop was full, people welcomed me, and I taught and performed. From then on, I was featured. I started getting more opportunities. My name began to get around."

Dancing on-one or on-two was not a source of disconnect beyond socials, where a dance might be rejected based on a difference of style. With thoughtful attention from incredible dancers like Sita and Addie, dancing on-one or on-two became a vehicle for inspiration and connection.

A Dance of Many Influences

The difference between dancing on-one or on-two points in Salsa's history. As we saw earlier, Salsa emerged as a blend of Afro-Caribbean dances that coalesced in New York in the 1930s, culminating in its rise in the 1970s. As Priscilla Renta describes in "Salsa Dance: Latino/a History in Motion," it was a potent combination of mambo, son, and the North American jazz and swing band era that set the scene for Salsa. These early mambo and son strains are where the distinctions among circular, on-one, and on-two Salsa originate, forming a topographical map of the origins and pathways of each style. Writing about these stylistic journeys in *Spinning Mambo Into Salsa*, Juliet McMains writes,

"Salsa of the 1970s departed from 1950s mambo on all three points—gravitation toward the downbeat, preference for partnered turns over solo footwork, and the frequent use of the cross-back basic—all of which could be linked (directly or indirectly) to the shifting social function of Salsa music as the voice of *el pueblo*."

In addition to these influences, as Salsa emerged as a dance and musical force in the latter half of the 1970s, the various strands of what was generally known as the hustle strongly impacted Salsa's growth and popularity. As Juan Flores notes in his book, *Salsa Rising: New York Latin Music of the Sixties Generation*, the hustle was more than just a fad.

"By the beginning of the decade, young Nuyoricans were already extending and veering off from the more traditional mambo-based Salsa style of their parents and creating a range of dance steps culminating in the hustle, soon referred to as the Latin hustle. Many of the fast moves, turns, and twirls associated with Salsa dancing of subsequent years were actually developed as part of the hustle, a chapter of New York Latin music as yet unanalyzed and in fact barely mentioned in the scant writing on the subject. While the origins of the hustle and related dance fads of those years clearly stem from African American choreographic histories, young Latinos assured an unmistakably Latin stylistic affiliation to the most enduring of the variants of the hustle, which is why like boogaloo before it and b-boying (breakdancing) thereafter, the 'Latin' epithet becomes so indispensable and definitional of the style as a whole."

As Salsa eventually gained popularity and left our communities in the 1990s, becoming something we learned and practiced in studios rather than clubs like the Palladium, these accents and stylistic choices served as a powerful echo of the many dance styles and moments of joyful resistance that went into the creation of this artistic language in the first place.

What Salsa Unlocked for Me

There's no way you could have told this four-year-old version of me that he would grow up to be a dancer. Sometimes it takes a little while to find your path.

I started my journey with Salsa as an observer: in my living room, as a five-year-old in the Bronx, looking at a Willie Colón album cover that portrayed him as a gangster, standing over a dead body with his trombone case held to evoke a gun; at my aunt's house as a ten-year-old in Guayama, holding that Ruben Blades album and poring over the translated lyrics. I was too young to understand all of the social commentary underneath the provocative imagery of those album covers. But I saw myself in them.

Eventually, I went from that little boy observing to the dancer performing, teaching, and transmitting Salsa culture to the next generation. It was me on the stages, me doing choreography, and me teaching the next generation to dance. I inherited a lineage and legacy, and I made it my mission to pass it along. In the process, my own internalized language ideology shifted completely.

Looking back with this new perspective, I realized that what mattered in my embarrassing Univision interview was not my proficiency but that I showed up for my students when it mattered. I brought Karla Cariño onto that stage, and I passed on our lineage and culture to hundreds, if not thousands, of students during my years working with Dancing Classrooms. That was the point.

And, as with so many things, once I let the shame go, things shifted with my relationship to Spanish. In fact, I had an opportunity to try a TV interview in Spanish again recently. I did things very differently, coming from a place of self-awareness and respect.

In 2018, my wife, Noni, had the opportunity to lead an independent school in Rhode Island. So we packed up and made the move up to Southern New England. After a few years in the Ocean State, I was happy to gain new friends and explore creative opportunities. I was a member of the Equity Leadership Initiative, a pilot program sponsored by the Rhode Island Foundation. It was a project intended to identify, develop, and network established and emerging leaders of color in Rhode Island. I applied and was accepted into the second cohort. I, along with 29 other leaders of color from across the state, took classes together, did enrichment and bonding exercises (including a Salsa class I had a blast leading), and engaged in leadership and professional development. Participants came from the private, public, nonprofit, and government sectors.

One of my friends in the group had become a reporter for a local news affiliate. She had launched a weekly news program devoted specifically to the Latino community in Rhode Island. The program would cover topics of interest to the Latino community and include interviews with community leaders. She asked whether I would be interested in being interviewed for one of these segments to discuss my work in dance.

My first question was, "Do I have to do this in Spanish?"

I was interviewed on a local TV news program in Rhode Island—in Spanish. Unlike my Univision experience, I approached this interview with greater confidence, if not with greater Spanish fluency.

She said I would have to do it in Spanish because it was for Spanish-speaking viewers. I explained that my Spanish was decent for conversation, but I was not comfortable with live television, as I had had some bad experiences. She asked what we could do. I suggested that if I could have the questions in advance, I could prepare my responses and feel more comfortable. She hesitated, but eventually agreed, with the caveat that I could not say the questions had been sent in advance, which was fine.

When it came time for the interview, Maria Elena, the lead correspondent, asked the prepared questions, but another reporter, Adriana, added a few unplanned ones. I was initially caught off guard, but the questions were simple and not overly technical. I responded, though not with the same level of precision as my prepared answers. But, at the end of the day, the interview went well, and I came away feeling solid about my performance. I had learned to set myself up for success.

My experience with dance impacted my relationship with language, because it was through dance that I began to reassess the ideology that held up my ideas around language. I saw that it was not an issue of my own capacity. Language, just like dance, was not "in my blood." I needed exposure, a playful attitude, dedication, and the right support to learn. And my belonging was always mine to define. In fact, by allowing the focus to stay on Spanish proficiency, accent, or the other things that have been used to divide me from myself, I was playing into the assimilationist playbook. Creating my own definition of Latinidad, allowing myself to feel and be fully Puerto Rican with or without Spanish, has been my defiant act of affirmation.

CHAPTER FOURTEEN

RAISING THE NEXT GENERATION

"Every time a person speaks, they embody an inherited chain of choices."

> —*Language City: The Fight to Preserve Endangered Mother Tongues in New York*, Ross Perlin

But Wait! There's More!

When my son Rodney Jr. (RJ) was born, he was the smallest baby I had ever seen. He was unbelievably cute. Today, you would never guess that the tall young man I am proud to call my son weighed less than five pounds at birth. I threw myself into the work of being his dad, and I wanted to do everything in my power to raise him to be proud of who he is. When my youngest son, Roman, was born less than two years later, I was once again left in awe of how perfect a tiny child could be, and I knew that it was my life's work to grow alongside these boys, guiding them as they came up in the world.

Parenthood always comes with challenges. But for some of us, it comes with a renewed shame from our childhood and early adulthood for not speaking the language that ties us to our roots.

Judy, my former partner and the wonderful mother of my two boys, is Dominican, and she grew up in Washington Heights and later in New Jersey, surrounded by Spanish. Unlike my parents and me, Judy spoke only Spanish at home, and her mother did not speak English. Getting to know Judy and raising the boys meant spending time with her parents, who didn't speak English. Whenever I visited their home, or they came to ours, I had to use all my Spanish to keep up, since Dominicans speak so fast. I often asked them to slow down or repeat themselves. Judy's mom, Dulce, was always kind and praised my Spanish, though I usually had to mix English and Spanish to get by. I was always a bit envious that Judy and her siblings were fully bilingual while my siblings and I weren't. Those pangs about Spanish seemed to have a way of showing up in these important moments in my life.

In New York, the first Sunday in June is unofficially Puerto Rican Day, thanks to the National Puerto Rican Day Parade. I celebrated at home with my boys when they were little guys.

Judy and I set the intention to teach our boys Spanish. We bought children's books in Spanish, sometimes in bilingual editions, and read to them regularly. We played both English and Spanish music at night and made sure to include Spanish-language programs on PBS whenever possible. We did what we could to create a bilingual environment. One practice that we began when they were very young (and continue to this day) is to hold hands prior to many of our meals and recite this short bilingual prayer: "It's nice to sit and eat with family. *Es bueno sentarse y comer con familia.* Thank you, God, for this food. Amen. *Gracias, Dios, por esta comida. Amen.*"

But the challenge was that Judy and I spoke to each other only in English. I've come to believe that the language parents use with each other matters deeply. In our household, English dominated, so the boys' first linguistic "downloads," so to speak, were all in English. Once they entered school, even at the pre-K and nursery level, everything reinforced that.

A much older Roman and Rodney Jr., celebrating Dominican pride with their mom, Judy.

For Judy and me, like many other parents, the end of our experience trying to include Spanish in our children's upbringing came when a professional suggested that we were confusing them, advice that is often outdated and inappropriate. When they were very young, the boys received at-home speech therapy. One of the speech therapists told us that speaking to the boys in both languages would confuse them and possibly delay their language development. These are the kinds of misconceptions that parents still hear and bias them against fostering a bilingual household.

We didn't have any dual-language programs in our neighborhood, which might have made a real difference. My sister-in-law and I have talked about that, and even in my interview with Jennifer Leeman, she pointed out how access to dual-language schooling could help shift language attitudes more broadly. Without it, though, it felt like pushing a rock uphill every day, just to see it back at the bottom again the next. A Sisyphean effort.

In addition to the structural issues, I soon saw that it is not as easy as simply deciding to speak Spanish to your children. If your child is about to jump off a table, you don't stop to think about what word to use in Spanish. You just yell "stop," because that's the language that comes naturally in the moment. So even with the best intentions, maintaining Spanish in the home becomes difficult. My boys are the third generation, and like clockwork, they've followed the familiar pattern of language loss.

As RJ and Roman grew, and it became clear that our lofty intentions had not been enough to produce Spanish fluency in either of them, I felt that familiar sense of shame. All the work I had done to feel whole and reassure myself that I could claim my own Latinidad became increasingly shaky as I realized I had not been able to make a different choice from the one my parents made. I felt ashamed, something Brené Brown describes as "the intensely painful feeling that we've been unjustly degraded, ridiculed, or put down and that our identity has been demeaned or devalued."

All of the times that my identity was questioned, I was mocked or ridiculed, or I felt I would never be fully claimed by anyone, flooded back to me. Adding to my own shame about my textbook Spanish was the sense of parental failure as a transmitter of our heritage language. But, as Brené Brown shows us, shame cannot live in the light. The more we talk to each other and share openly what troubles us, the less power our shame holds over us. That is exactly what happened to me, and it was especially evident during the process of interviewing experts, friends, colleagues, and family for this book. The stories about parenting underscored something very powerful: It isn't just me, and it isn't just you struggling with this. By sharing our experiences, we lighten our own burden and create a space where dreaming of a different future becomes possible.

When Expectations Meet Reality

"In studying language dynamics, how are we to know if we are witnessing the maintenance of Spanish or just a stage in the path toward its loss?"

—*Household Perspectives on Minority Language Maintenance and Loss: Language in the Small Spaces*, by Isabel Velázquez

As I spoke with members of my family, friends, colleagues, experts, and others who shared stories about raising bilingual children, the patterns were clear. So many of us go into the situation thinking we have more power to choose than we really do. In reality, the assimilationist forces and dominance of English in the U.S. make it an uphill battle, and one we rarely win at the third generation or beyond. By clearly naming the structural elements conspiring against us, we are not only able to release our own shame, but we give ourselves the space to envision a different future for the generations to come, one where the structures around us support multilingualism and genuine multiculturalism.

Throughout these powerful stories, I return to the framework introduced in Chapter Three by Pilar Garces-Conejo Blitvich, which helps us understand not only why none of us achieved complete success in passing Spanish on to the next generation, but also how that manifests in our families.

Garces-Conejo Blitvich defines five different profiles or orientations toward the issue of not speaking Spanish, and I have found these different models helpful as I have spoken with dozens of people about their experiences. I also recognize that I have fallen into a few of these categories at different times in my own life. The categories can almost be seen as a spectrum, and they show up in different configurations and combinations at the same time. The first profile, "Enoughness," refers to a person with enough fluency to be deemed "authentically" Latino. The second, the "Neoliberal Views" profile, appears when the individual centers themselves and believes it is up to them, not institutions or "white hegemony," to change. In the third type, "Emotion," we see a strong emotional response to language, including the range of challenging emotions many of us feel about not being proficient in our heritage language. With the "Critical Views" profile, fourth on the list, institutions and "white hegemony" are seen as the barrier to access to the language. And the last profile, "Essentialism," holds that "there is an intrinsic connection between language and identity."

In my exploration of this topic, I have found these profiles resonant, though I think many of us move fluidly among them at different times in our lives. People tend to be a little militant when they are younger, but as I got older and became a parent, I softened my stance because life experience taught me to do so. I don't think that if you're aligning with the neoliberal profile in your 20s, you will necessarily retain that point of view in your 50s, especially if you've become a parent. Life might teach you some things.

Some families can successfully pass Spanish on to their children, perhaps even to the third generation. However, for most families, this is an uphill battle and often requires time, financial, and relational resources that most families simply don't have access to. The abundance of apps and online language courses makes basic language learning more accessible, but higher-order fluency still requires immersion and frequency of practice that can place such fluency out of reach.

The Sanchez-Jackson Family

Lydia Sanchez is a longtime friend and dance partner who has built a successful career as a paralegal across a variety of corporate and other settings. I had the pleasure of interviewing her and her three children, who ranged in age from thirteen to twenty when we spoke. The three children described their passions, projects, and dreams for the future with infectious energy before our conversation shifted to Spanish. The older two kids agreed they could understand a lot and get by with basic Spanish vocabulary when spending time in Puerto Rico or Colombia, but they don't really speak it fluently. Caleb, the youngest of the three, described his exposure to Spanish growing up as limited to the Salsa, bachata, and merengue his mom liked to listen to, and he said he can't understand or speak it.

This dynamic, with eldest children getting more exposure and younger siblings getting less, is very common, as is the reality that by the second and definitely the third generation, gaining proficiency is not likely.

Lydia grew up in New York in a Puerto Rican family, learning Spanish with extended family members who did not speak English:

> "I was my grandmother's interpreter for as long as I can remember. I was four years old in the hospital with her, translating for the doctor because my mother couldn't be there. My grandmother wasn't fluent in English, so I, along with my brother and sister, interpreted for her for many years."

When it came time to raise her own family, Lydia intended to speak to her children in Spanish and provide them with as much exposure to the language as possible. Even little things like the Puerto Rican greeting *bendición*, meaning blessings, were part of what she wanted to pass down. Lydia described feeling happy and relieved to find a Puerto Rican babysitter, and to ensure her two eldest children had enough exposure to Spanish to speak to their grandparents in it.

But when we look at the maintenance of Spanish in second and third-generation migrant or immigrant families, another factor to consider is exogamy, or marrying outside of our culture. In *Speaking Spanish in the US: The Sociopolitics of Language*, Fuller and Leeman cite rising rates of exogamy, especially among U.S.-born Latinos. In 2015, 39% of U.S.-born Latinos were marrying non-Latinos. This is significant because Fuller and Leeman also note that the rate of parents speaking Spanish to their children drops from 92% when both parents are Latino to 55% when only one parent is Latino.

In Lydia's family, her ex-husband is African American and did not come from a Latino background. His lack of Spanish became a barrier that Lydia and her children could not overcome. While he had been initially supportive of her speaking Spanish to the children, something changed when the two eldest were preschoolers, and Caleb had yet to be born:

"When I met my ex-husband, I made it clear I wanted our children to speak Spanish. At first, he agreed, but from one moment to the next, he became very angry and jealous about it. Abuelo Juan, a father figure to me, would visit our house unannounced, often building things for the kids, like a desk. One day, he came over and built a desk while my ex-husband was at work. When he saw it, he was upset. He said he didn't want

Abuelo Juan speaking Spanish to the children, or for the children to speak Spanish at all, because he didn't know the language.

He had even learned a few Spanish phrases from being around us, but it became a source of conflict in our marriage. I had to choose between staying married and continuing to speak Spanish to my children. I chose to stay married, and that meant denying a part of my culture. For years, the kids only heard Spanish at family gatherings, and I couldn't speak to my parents or family in Spanish when he was home.

One of my biggest regrets is not standing firm on this. I remember taking the kids to Mexico, where they met other children and felt sad and embarrassed that they couldn't speak Spanish fluently. That silence lasted until Caleb was about seven. It was heartbreaking to see the cultural connection I valued so much compromised, and it remains a deep disappointment in my life."

This left Shai, Ariel, and Caleb without enough exposure to become proficient in Spanish, and they report the same feelings of isolation, shame, and longing that many of us feel as a result. While they did have some opportunity to study Spanish at school, the lost momentum from their early years had a big impact, and the later exposure was not enough to make up for it.

Ariel, who did get exposure to Spanish in her preschool years, described her relationship to the language now in the following way:

"Sometimes I'm able to keep up, sometimes I'm not. When I'm with family at the Christmas party on my mom's side in upstate New York, a lot of them speak Spanish. Some understand English, so I'll try to speak to them in English, but if not, I almost *put up a front* [italics mine] that I know Spanish to a certain extent. I don't want to look like a complete loser. I'll speak Spanglish a little, incorporate small words I know, or make short sentences. Usually, I can get away with it, whether I understand them or not. I just try to find the keywords in what they're saying and piece it together in my mind. Some words I just know as soon as I hear them, without even thinking."

Shai, the eldest, described an experience that was very relatable to me, despite the fact that he is in the same age group as my sons. I can remember running lists of verb conjugations or trying to recall drills from Spanish class. In fact, I still feel that way when speaking my textbook version of Spanish, and I feel a good deal of empathy for Shai, whose opportunity to learn Spanish as a kid was cut short:

"I really do feel left out because I've always dreamed of speaking another language, especially Spanish. I'd love to be fluent, or at least know enough words and sentences to feel like I fit in. Sometimes when people are speaking Spanish, I know what they're talking about, and I pause, trying to remember what words I know from the classes I took. I think about how to say the right conjugation, how to form a sentence, but it takes time. While I'm still trying to figure it out, they keep talking, and I end up getting nowhere. Eventually, I just give up and speak in English."

Caleb, who was not raised with any Spanish at home and is still a young teen, had deep insight into how not having access to the language makes him feel and how he has consciously built a mindset of connection without it:

"For me, my feelings about my family speaking Spanish, or even just my mom speaking Spanish, are very different from my older brother's and sister's. When I moved here [relocated from Long Island to New Jersey], I had only taken two years of Spanish classes before switching to French, though now I'm switching back to Spanish. Like Ariel mentioned, we go to family parties, especially on Christmas Eve, where everyone, our aunts, uncles, and cousins, is speaking Spanish. I've gotten used to knowing that I can't fully communicate with them on that level.

One thing I've always envied about my mom is her ability to walk into any place, a family gathering or a restaurant, and start speaking Spanish right away, just knowing someone else speaks it. For me, it's not so much a mental strain anymore as it is an awareness I've come to accept. Even though I don't speak Spanish, I still really love the culture. I love Puerto Rico, the islands, the music, and the food, and I feel like that passion balances out not being part of the group in my family who speaks Spanish."

Ivelisse Garcia

Another story I heard about exogamy came from my former colleague, Ivelisse Garcia. Ivelisse was born in Puerto Rico and came to the U.S. for college, at which point she did not speak fluent English. She put down roots in the U.S. and eventually married a white man, although they later divorced. She told me about her experience trying to teach her eldest child Spanish, saying:

"We planned to teach both kids Spanish, but it didn't happen. My children understand a little, but they're uncomfortable speaking it. I would speak Spanish with my son during the day, but when his dad came home, we switched to English because my ex didn't know Spanish.

In a household where both parents speak Spanish, it can be the default at home, and the child learns English at school. For us, switching languages confused my son. When he reached milestones, he wasn't speaking as expected, and I blamed myself. I didn't have family nearby and was a first-time mother.

I decided to stick to one language to reduce confusion, which was the wrong choice. Now we know bilingual kids often start speaking later but catch up quickly. At the time, I just did what I thought was best with the information I had."

Elizabeth Ramirez

My friend since childhood, Liz, told me how her circumstances prevented her from even trying to teach her kids Spanish at home. Her former partner is Irish, but they separated, and she raised her kids as a single parent:

"It wasn't intentional, but I didn't emphasize Spanish with my kids because I was busy being a nurse, a single mom, and managing everything else. I focused on being a good mom rather than teaching Spanish.

My grandparents did speak Spanish to the kids, teaching them little words and phrases here and there, but it wasn't structured or meaningful. At the time, I didn't feel it was as important as everything else I needed to focus on.

Today, Rebecca understands some Spanish because she spends time at my grandfather's house helping care for him. Though he has dementia, speaking Spanish to him calms him and helps him understand better than English, which has required Rebecca to learn more Spanish."

Verónica Guevara

Bilingual educator Verónica Guevara comes from a Mexican-American and Puerto Rican household in Houston, Texas. She married a white man who didn't speak Spanish, and she explained how a combination of factors we have already seen in previous stories—single parenthood, a busy schedule, and the intensity of English dominance around her children—made it hard for her to fulfill her goal of raising Spanish-speaking children:

"I focused on teaching my children Spanish and spoke it exclusively to Tomás until he was about three, when he began asking for English after preschool. I started mixing both languages and did the same with Elena, though after my divorce and return to work, it became harder to keep up.

I taught Spanish at the Quaker school they attended, and they were proud their mother spoke another language. Even if they never became fluent, they understand a lot and see it as part of who they are.

Tomás married a woman adopted from Guatemala who wants to learn Spanish. My daughter hopes to travel with me to Spain. Their father and I chose names that reflected their heritage but were simple for others—Tomás and Elena. Still, people often struggle with them.

Now my children are adults with a blend of Irish, Swedish, Mexican, Puerto Rican, and Minnesotan roots. English may have taken over, but Spanish still lives in them."

My Nephews, Joey and Jordan Nieves, and Second Cousin, Chris Baldwin

When I spoke with several of my relatives about this recently, they shared insights into their experiences growing up in second-generation households.

My second cousin Chris Baldwin with his mom, my cousin, Jessica Colón-Baldwin. Chris is the family's intrepid traveler. Jessica is one of the best Spanish speakers in my generational cohort.

My second cousin Chris Baldwin told us an interesting story about stepping out of his comfort zone and using his Spanish in situations where he had little choice. His grandmother (my Titi Sonia), who is bilingual, has begun speaking to him rapidly in Spanish as her condition has declined in a nursing home, so Chris has been forced to expand his ability to both understand and respond. He described similar experiences traveling and how much immersion has helped him improve.

Jordan and Joey, my sister Leslie's sons, talked about their experiences as young fathers. Their dad is very fluent in Spanish but was focused on English and did not speak Spanish to his kids growing up, and their mom, my sister Leslie, was only able to speak Spanglish to her kids.

My niece, Elisa, alongside her brothers, my nephews, Jordan and Joey Nieves. Despite not speaking Spanish at home, Joey and Jordan continue to look for ways to transmit Spanish to their children.

Now, as parents themselves, Jordan and Joey have not given up on Spanish. Knowing what it is like to be Puerto Rican and only speak English, they hope to provide at least a bit more exposure to their children than they had. Addressing the issue head-on, Joey asked his dad to speak Spanish to the grandchildren, and he has had some limited success. Jordan found a Spanish-speaking babysitter, a strategy we saw work well for Lydia in her early success. Jordan wisely reflected on the situation, saying:

> "Dad speaks to Kristina in Spanish a little, and Mom does too, but her babysitter speaks Spanish all the time. We asked her to use Spanish as much as possible, so she's always hearing it. So she still has a better opportunity than we did."

I am proud of my nephews for their efforts. While the circumstances and structures around them do not support full bilingualism, it is commendable that they provide their young children with as much exposure as possible. In a second- or third-generation migrant household, even a small amount of Spanish will make a difference in their children's sense of belonging.

Every Time a Person Speaks

The choice many of my friends, family, and colleagues tried to make—the choice to try to speak and transmit Spanish to our children despite the odds being against us—was never isolated. Our intentions and our efforts were not in vain, and our lack of success does not take away from the love we showed to ourselves and our culture by placing enough importance on Spanish to at least try. In the face of insidious pressure to assimilate, our efforts needed the perfect combination of factors, all based on luck and resources, to be effective. Describing the intensity of the pressure to focus solely on English, Ross Perlin writes:

> "It can be profoundly useful to be a native speaker of the dominant dialect of a dominant language. Representing the associated 'mainstream' culture with every sound means being able to talk to many and sound good to most, set above the particulars of region, class, or ethnicity, though also lacking those solidarities. Rarely does a dominant-language monolingual need to speak anyone else's language, and it counts as a charming attempt if they do, a mark of open-mindedness and sophistication or an advanced party trick. A person 'without an accent' is by default considered to be smarter or better educated as soon as they open their mouth."

Every time we open our mouths to speak, even in the privacy of our own homes, we are joining the choir of historical, political, and personal choices that lead to the current moment. The household and intimate realms are where minority languages survive and grow, according to Isabel Velázquez in her work *Household Perspectives on Minority Language Maintenance and Loss: Language in the Small Spaces*, but that does not mean they are apolitical or unaffected by dominant narratives and language ideologies. She goes on to describe the fight to maintain minority languages, writing, "Ultimately, language maintenance is part of a broader power struggle, which is mostly fought through discourses around language."

The Third Generation

"Historically, immigrants to the U.S. have largely followed a three-generation pattern of language shift to English, with the immigrant generation being mostly dominant in the non-English language, the second generation being bilingual, and the third (and subsequent) generations being monolingual in English."
—*Speaking Spanish in the U.S.: The Sociopolitics of Language,*
by Janet M. Fuller and Jennifer Leeman

My sons and nephews and many of the children my friends and colleagues spoke about in this chapter are all part of the third generation. As we have seen across multiple sources, the third generation shows the most definitive loss of Spanish (or any other language from another country). Factors like grandparents or parents who don't speak English and the influence of strong ties to the home country fade, and the power of English only grows.

We must wonder what this means for the future of Latinidad in the U.S., as "demographers predict that between 2006 and 2050 the Latino student population will grow by 166%, compared to four percent among other groups," according to Allard, Mortimer, Gallo, Link, and Wortham in *Immigrant Spanish as Liability or Asset? Generational Diversity in Language Ideologies at School.* With this population growth increasingly driven by third generations and beyond, it is time for us to ask the big questions about Spanish. If other nations with significant exposure to multiple languages have embraced the benefits of multilingualism and made space for minority languages to flourish across generations, providing cognitive and cultural benefits across society, why can't we?

CHAPTER FIFTEEN

HEALING THROUGH FATHERHOOD

"Despite their original intentions, parents in multilingual households need to re-evaluate their approach as life situations and family needs change over time. This is, of course, a point well understood by any parent attempting to raise young children, regardless of linguistic environment."

—*Household Perspectives on Minority Language Maintenance and Loss: Language in the Small Spaces*, by Isabel Velázquez

My Younger Sister Speaks Spanish

Becoming a father was not the only stage in my life when the old language wound reopened. When I was in high school, my parents divorced, and my mother remarried a few years later. Around the time I finished college at 20, my mom brought my little sister, Alexa, into the world. She was a lovely baby, and I was pleased for my mom, though I wasn't at a stage in life when I expected to welcome a baby sibling. But there was something even more unexpected waiting for me.

After Alexa was born, I would visit my mother, and from the moment I walked in, she would start speaking to me in Spanish as if we had always communicated that way. There was never a setup, never a conversation establishing that she had shifted strategies and wanted me to participate in my sister's Spanish-immersive childhood, even though I was not a confident Spanish speaker, given my English upbringing. It felt as if, overnight, Mom had switched to speaking Spanish with no preamble.

Mom, enjoying a laugh with my baby sister, Alexa Flores. Alexa was a beautiful addition to the family. I just wasn't prepared for the change in mom's attitude toward speaking Spanish.

At first, I felt dislocated, awkward, and unsure. What felt surprising and attention-grabbing at first eventually felt a little hurtful and even insensitive, because she wouldn't budge. I kept responding in English. I wasn't trying to speak Spanish; I was digging in, thinking it wasn't the right time to practice. I stubbornly decided that since she hadn't taught Spanish to me, I wouldn't be participating in her latent Spanish-only household project in my twenties. With greater maturity and forgiveness, I probably could have seen it as an opportunity to practice, but I wasn't at that place.

Even years later, when I call my mom, she initiates conversation with me in Spanish, and I respond in English. Now it feels like a game we play. But we have had some helpful conversations recently, and I understand why she did what she did, both with Alexa and me. Becoming a parent myself also helped me understand how hard this is, even with the best intentions.

My mom, Margie, described the difference between raising me and raising Alexa, explaining that she had gained maturity and life experience, and she saw Spanish as a "necessity" for Alexa. In contrast, she had been hyper-focused on my learning English as a newly arrived migrant and first-time mother. She saw the value in Spanish, and it felt natural to speak it at home, as it was not in the household where I was raised.

It took some time and becoming a parent myself, but I was eventually able to make peace with my parents' choices around Spanish. Language transmission is difficult and requires lots of support.

Although I have a lot of grace for the situation now, at the time, it felt intensely frustrating and even painful. I had a chip on my shoulder, and it took a lot of growth to shed the resentment I carried.

Why was Alexa being given this golden ticket to Latinidad, to belonging, to being Puerto Rican that had been kept from me? It reinforced a deep sense of the whole situation being personal, being a failure on my part, or some kind of flaw within me. My mom made a different choice with my sister, showing me that she could have made a different choice with me, but she hadn't. The shame and resentment I felt stemmed from my lack of intragroup acceptance, something Pilar Garces-Conejo Blitvich connects firmly to Spanish proficiency for Latinos in the U.S. in her work, *"You are shamed for speaking it or for not speaking it good enough": The paradoxical status of Spanish in the U.S. Latino Community*:

> "Due to Spanish having been regarded as the foundation of Latinidad, Latinos who are unable to speak Spanish see this lack of ability as a major hindrance for intragroup acceptance. Findings of their two studies revealed that (1) "Spanish speaking inability was associated with greater perceived intragroup rejection, lower collective self-esteem, and less felt similarity to other Latinos" and (2) "when Latinos' inability to speak Spanish was revealed to a fellow Latino, they are less likely to categorise themselves as Latinos and also indicate lower private regard and less felt connectedness to other Latinos."

My private shame, the way I felt like an American high school student, not the Puerto Rican man I longed to be when I spoke Spanish, clung to me. Learning how widespread these feelings are, as shown by Garces and the many other researchers whose work has so richly informed this book, has certainly been a piece in the puzzle of releasing these feelings and moving toward a new paradigm of wholeness. But, in those moments, entering my mother's belated Spanish-only household as a young man and non-Spanish speaker, I felt torn up inside. I deeply identified with Natasha Alford, the author of *American Negra*, a memoir partly about her experiences growing up as the daughter of an African American father and a Puerto Rican mother. Regarding the tension she experienced with her mother over Spanish, Natasha writes:

> "The more I encountered judgment in the world for not being fluent in Spanish, the more I resented that Mami didn't teach it to me. How could I fully be my mother's daughter if there were conversations we could never have? For every bit of pure love she'd poured into me, she didn't give me the one thing that she was best positioned to give me: her language."

The "Mother" Tongue

> "Childrearing is a gendered endeavor precisely because it is socially constructed. Care, affection, and intergenerational transmission are related to a particular idea of motherhood centered on a specific set of social expectations of women. What is important for the intergenerational transmission of a minority language, then, is not maternal engagement conceived simply as women's work, but rather the household presence of an adult figure who fulfills the expectations socially attributed to women."
>
> —*Household Perspectives on Minority Language Maintenance and Loss: Language in the Small Spaces*, by Isabel Velázquez

When I reflect on my mom's experience, it is interesting to realize that she was only 17 years old when she migrated to the U.S. Having spent her childhood working constantly, providing childcare for her many younger siblings, she did not have a lot of time for herself. I know she loved school, but it was not something her life circumstances allowed her to focus on. Instead, she migrated to New York after a family tragedy left her bereft and in need of a change, something a relative who was already in New York was able to offer her.

Mom did learn some English at school, but the way she was taught didn't allow her to communicate fluently upon arrival in New York. So her focus during those first decades in a new country was on English. I imagine she was eager to adapt and threw herself into assimilating into her new home.

My wife, Noni, and I enjoying a fun dance moment at an outdoor Salsa social in New York City. Dance brought us together and allows us to speak our own personal language.

My lovely wife, Noni, whom I had the joy and privilege of marrying in 2014, is also an educator and now the head of one of New York City's most prestigious independent schools. She comes from a similar background to my own in some ways. Her mom, Marcia, is Puerto Rican, though she was born and raised in the U.S. Interestingly, she was experiencing many of the same feelings I was, even though she had dealt with them a generation earlier.

In her early childhood, she lived in an extended family structure that provided her with a lot of exposure, but her family moved to Texas when she was still young, due to her adoptive father's military service. Moving back to New York, Marcia described an experience that surprised me, because it could have happened in the 80s or 2000s, but it happened in the 60s:

"When my father started doing really well, we moved to Yonkers. And then I went to Catholic school. Our Lady of Fatima. Now I remember that. And that's at the point where people were sort of mocking us because these were like rich white kids. I mean, I was in class with the vice president of the Yankees' kid, and the Dodgers were still in New York, and the general manager of the Dodgers' kid was in the class. We were nowhere near that. [I was a] butcher's child. So that's when my father decided he wanted to Americanize us, and he stopped speaking Spanish. So that's where I lost it. Now I can understand it like my aunts would. They talked to me in Spanish, and I could understand them, and I couldn't reply. Does that make sense? Of course it does. So even to this day, they would talk to me in Spanish, and I know what they're saying, but I can't get the sentences and paragraphs together to reply back to them in Spanish. So I just replied in English, and it was fine with them."

Just as my mom chose to focus on my English acquisition due to assimilationist pressures, my mother-in-law's family was going through a similar process a generation earlier. Within a rigid, monolingual, white supremacist culture, the dynamism of a bilingual childhood was a liability, not an asset.

Marcia married an African American man and moved to North Carolina with him in 1974, which she said was terrifying. She knew that a mixed-race marriage could be a very dangerous thing, and she focused on raising her kids in a proud, afro-centric environment to support them in the face of racist policies and communities that she knew would harm them if they were not well-prepared, although she worried that no preparation would be good enough.

Even though she is very proud to be Puerto Rican, Marcia was not able to focus on creating avenues for connection with her culture for Noni and her younger brothers, Jamal and Sharif. She was able to expose them to some music and food, but she expressed guilt and regret about not being able to teach them any Spanish or raise them in Puerto Rican culture.

> "I didn't introduce that language to them, because it had more or less been taken away from me. I felt really guilty about that. As my daughter will tell you, I'm very proud of being Puerto Rican. I see Puerto Ricans everywhere."

Marcia's story, my mom's story, and many of the stories in the previous chapter reflect something that needs to be named: the role of mother in language learning, and the tremendous burden many mothers carry in nurturing cultural and linguistic belonging. It is no accident that we call a person's native language their "mother tongue." Although it is not an excuse for fathers, Janet M. Fuller and Jennifer Leeman state very bluntly that "mothers seem to play a more important role in intergenerational transmission than do fathers." This is yet another example of how we have allowed language transmission to flounder without the support it needs. Mothers, you should not be doing this alone.

Like my mom, my mother-in-law, Marcia Thomas, had a complicated relationship with Spanish in New York City. Here, she's enjoying her grandson Novian's graduation from law school along with her children Noni, Jamal, and Sharif.

Fathers: An Invitation

My son Rodney Jr. takes great pride in his Puerto Rican and Dominican heritage, displaying the Puerto Rican flag at a Providence College campus event.

When I reflect on my own experience and role as a father to RJ and Roman, I do not see failure, even when I think of the difference between our expectations and the reality of raising bilingual children. Instead, I feel affirmed when I remember sending our eldest son off to Providence College, a predominantly white school, only to see him graduate as president of the Multicultural Club, lead the Latin American Student Organization, and collaborate with the Black Student Organization. Roman has always maintained a strong affection for his Dominican and Puerto Rican heritage, soaking up as much as he can about the Caribbean's geography and relishing his visits there. He has always wanted to learn as much Spanish as possible and often prompts us to practice. At the end of the day, I know I could have done more, but if my sons feel proud to be Afro-Latino, if they feel grounded in who they are, that's what matters.

My son Roman has always been a natural mover. Here he is keeping up with his old man at a holiday dance event at the Winter Garden, where PS 115 won the Grand Finals years earlier.

Raising my boys helped me make sense of what happened during my own childhood, and it gave me a reason to get really clear on who I am. I would never have allowed anyone to tell my children that they did not belong or that they could not claim their own identity as Afro-Latinos because they speak the wrong colonial language. Yet, I had allowed people to make me feel less than. By providing this solid base for my boys, I was finally able to integrate what I had learned through Salsa. There is never just one path to belonging.

What mattered most, at the end of the day, was the conversations we had around the table and the sense of pride Judy and I modeled and spoke clearly into being for our children.

If you are a father or a man involved in the lives of younger family members or community members, I want to speak directly to you.

We all have a role to play in changing the language ideology that has kept Latinos and other multilingual or immigrant communities stuck in cycles of shame that only serve the greater goal of assimilation. In facing our feelings, finding ways to build healthy identities, and continuing to fight for our minority languages, even when it is hard, we are working to shift the narrative. It is important that we shoulder our fair share of the burden, reflect deeply on these issues, engage in care labor, and serve as positive mentors.

Bilingual Education: A Roadmap

Bilingual education in New York, in particular, has made incredible strides over the past several decades, thanks to the tireless work of educators, advocates, community members, and elected officials. But the timeline shows just how long it takes for systemic change to reach students. The groundwork began in the late 1960s and early 1970s with the establishment of the New York State Office of Bilingual Education in 1969 and the recognition of bilingual education as a formal instructional tool. In 1974, the same year I was born, the ASPIRA consent decree guaranteed New York City students the right to transitional bilingual education and English as a Second Language. This landmark moment helped set the stage and, in many ways, mirrors the differences between my sister Alexa, who is 20 years younger, and my own.

It took another twenty years for the first Spanish-English dual-language program to open in Washington Heights in 1996, showing that even when the legal foundation exists, schools take time to innovate and grow, and in that interim, kids still navigate the challenges of learning a new language without formal support.

Since then, New York City has continued to expand its dual language offerings, creating forty new programs for the 2015–2016 school year and launching the first South Asian program in Bengali in 2018. The work of bilingual educators, administrators, and activists has been foundational to these advances, and I deeply appreciate their dedication to fostering a bilingual society.

But schools are only one front in this effort. What we have seen from families, communities, and our own experiences is that language development happens in a larger ecosystem, shaped not just by policy but by daily practice, community support, and cultural connection. The advocacy, care, and expertise of these educators have created essential opportunities for generations of students, and for that work, we owe a tremendous thanks. The change we see in New York is a roadmap for communities and families across the United States. When we place value on Spanish and other minority languages, we allow ourselves to be whole.

Healing the Language Wound

In *American Negra*, Natasha Alford describes the sense of inadequacy and shame that comes with not speaking our language, even if we know we didn't have much of a chance:

> "'Oh, that's a shame she doesn't know,' one Latina woman remarked to my mother about me not speaking Spanish, when we were visiting Puerto Rican friends on the West Side. Mamí did her usual apologetic explaining about how it was her fault that I didn't speak Spanish, but it was me who felt the transference of energy and humiliation."

While my fluency in Salsa gave me an embodied sense of my own identity, it was fatherhood that prompted me to begin shedding the shame of not speaking Spanish. I began to unravel the language ideologies that had been passed down to me; ideas that I had even taken on as my own.

I shifted "You can't be a *real* Puerto Rican if you don't speak the right kind of Spanish" into "I fit into my cultural and ethnic lineage perfectly, and I can be many things at once." In trying to give the gift of belonging to my boys, I received it as well.

Knowing that shame is social gives us a powerful tool because, as Brené Brown writes in *Atlas of the Heart: Mapping Meaningful Connection and the Language of Human Experience*:

> "Shame is a social emotion. Shame happens between people, and it heals between people. Even if I feel it alone, shame is the way I see myself through someone else's eyes. Self-compassion is often the first step to healing shame—we need to be kind to ourselves before we can share our stories with someone else."

Language shame provides us with an especially potent case for healing in community because language is fundamentally about connection. According to the Pew Research Center, just over half of non-Spanish-speaking Hispanics have been shamed by other Hispanics for not speaking Spanish. So the problem and, to some degree, the solution reside within our own community. When we refuse to hide, when we share our feelings about our heritage language openly, and when we shift our culture away from mocking and belittling Latinos whose Spanish is not perfect, we are healing the shame and pushing back against assimilation. And we know that positive interactions, reinforcement, and acceptance are what people of all ages require for learning. We must allow learning to unfold in a context of safety, playfulness, and encouragement, allowing our learners to become masterful at making the many mistakes they will need to make along the path to mastery.

Shifting our thinking in this way represents a revolutionary shift in our language ideology, but I believe we can bring this change. With over 40 million Latinos in the U.S. today, I invite you to claim your space. Spanish is an American language, too, and multilingualism is a healthy and generative facet of our society that should be supported and uplifted at all levels, from the teenager stumbling over grammar in a heritage language to the code-switching *tias*.

Language ideologies form the basis for "connections between language and people, connections that have implications about who people are, what they are worth, and how they should be treated," according to Elaine Allard and her colleagues. It is high time we countered the colonial language ideologies of perfectionism and monolingualism that we inherited with something that better reflects the syncretic, vibrant, resilient reality of who we are as Latinos in the U.S.

DINING ROOM SPANISH

"One of the mistakes I see language learners make is believing that studying languages is about acquiring knowledge. It's not! Learning a new language is about building a communication skill."

—Benny Lewis, polyglot

Back on Campus and Sharing Our Cultural Belonging Through Dance

When RJ was a senior at Providence College, I had one of the most gratifying experiences of my life. He was deeply involved in campus cultural life, becoming president of the Multicultural Society and a member of the Latin American Student Union. Even though Providence is a predominantly white school, he found his community and a sense of belonging, which I thought was fantastic.

At one point, his group was organizing events for the clubs, and someone suggested hosting a dance class. Of course, my son said, "I know a guy."

I will never forget the surreal, wonderful feeling of teaching my son and his peers a series of dance classes at his college. It was a beautiful, full-circle moment. From learning my first steps with my mom in order to present Salsa at my high school's multicultural night, to teaching my son's Multicultural Society a series of dance classes at Providence, I felt like I had completed a cycle in my life that was deeply healing.

Gratifying full-circle moment getting to teach Salsa and bachata to Rodney Jr.'s friends at Providence College.

Learning Is Possible: Play and Embracing Discomfort

Playfulness is essential to learning new skills, especially as an adult. I try to infuse my teaching with joy, as I did at this family dance event at Thayer Academy in Massachusetts.

As I reflect on my experiences with language shame, learning my heritage language as an additional language in high school, learning to dance, and becoming a dance teacher, I see many threads that weave the two pieces of my life together: dance and language. In both cases, it was the ability to engage playfully, make mistakes, feel supported, and have sufficient opportunities to practice with others that enabled learning. Identity is something we build with the people around us, as we speak, or dance our way to belonging.

I wholeheartedly believe in the power of arts education, and I have witnessed the transformative community that dance can create. "Dance is emerging as a vital tool to maintain the balance between what's going on in the body and how that feeds into our experience of life," according to Caroline Williams in *Move: How the New Science of Body Movement Can Set Your Mind Free*. When we step into our own bodies, onto the dance floor, and into motion with our dance partners, we are stepping into community with ourselves.

This sense of belonging provides the foundation for us to build a tolerance for discomfort and a tolerance for making mistakes, which are both crucial for learning. Our brain is a connection and prediction-making machine, and it doesn't "care about filling in bubbles on standardized tests or heated debates about curricular assessments. Our brain is structured to build new connections and to constantly evolve, and how we learn is not the same as a societal education system too often built around memorization of rote data and recall," Susan Magsamen and Ivy Ross write in *Your Brain on Art: How the Arts Transform Us*. So it is no wonder that the arts, and social dance in particular, have this incredible power to show us how to learn, bringing our whole selves to the task.

Dance showed me that learning was possible. It showed me that my identity was not limited by what I was given in childhood, and it allowed me to feel a deep sense of belonging. More importantly, it allowed me to see that there was nothing wrong with me, nothing fundamentally holding me back from learning Spanish. It was never me or my fault; I simply had not been afforded the opportunity to put in my ten thousand hours and "make more mistakes than others make attempts," a key element of learning, according to Adam Grant.

For decades, I believed it was too late for me. I had internalized the idea that if you don't learn a language in early childhood, you will never achieve fluency. And I let the shame I felt hold me back from even trying, but Adam Grant writes, "Polyglots prove that it's possible to master new languages well into adulthood … It was because they cleared a motivational hurdle: they got comfortable being uncomfortable," in *Hidden Potential: The Science of Achieving Greater Things*.

Continuing to provide us with a helpful reframe for language acquisition, Adam Grant describes how a polyglot he interviewed, Benny Lewis, was successful after he intentionally set out to make **200 mistakes a day**:

> "Along the way, Benny has put himself in some awkward positions. He's introduced himself with the wrong gender, said he was attracted to a bus, and accidentally complimented someone for having a nice arse. But he doesn't beat himself up, because his goal is to make mistakes. Even when he fumbles, people generally commend him for making an effort. And that motivates him to keep trying.

> Psychologists call that cycle learned industriousness. When you get praised for making an effort, the feeling of effort itself starts to take on secondary reward properties. Instead of having to push yourself to keep trying, you feel pulled toward it."

You are enough just as you are, and you are a Latino or Latina regardless of what level of Spanish you speak. But if you want to work on your Spanish, it is never too late to get back in the sandbox, play around, and make mistakes.

You Are Enough

If you have ever been made to feel like you are *not* enough, I hope that my story has helped you contextualize this and feel more able to see the structural factors that have made us feel this way. It may seem like common sense that the United States is a monolingual, English-speaking country. However, we do not have to accept this "zero-sum relationship" in which "languages other than English are constructed as inherently un-

American and threatening to English as well as to national identity," as noted by Jennifer Leeman. In fact, this zero-sum mentality has caused immeasurable harm to migrants and immigrants since the foundation of this nation, and arguably since ancient times, but we can center ourselves in our lineages of resistance, refuse to internalize this idea that we are not enough just as we are, and embody the resilient joy of our ancestors.

Just as Salsa showed me that resistance is best performed with joy, your very existence can stand as a rebuke to assimilation. By refusing to allow your identity to be flattened, packaged, and neatly categorized, you can create breathing space for yourself and the generations to come. When I am dancing, I always think of my ancestors, from sugarcane fields and the Palladium to well-worn kitchens in the Caribbean and in New York, dancing a path for me.

Full Circle Moments

My younger son, Roman, has always been good at relationships, close to his family, and focused on connection. A few years ago, inspired by his interest in improving his Spanish, I signed up for a course that the three of us ended up taking together at my kitchen table in Rhode Island.

I bought this online course called Speak Spanish Faster, by an instructor named Rocky Rodriguez, a Puerto Rican from New York who wanted to teach people like me how to learn Spanish quickly. During the shift to remote learning during COVID, we lost a lot, but we also gained opportunities like this one, where courses went online, and we could learn from our own homes.

At one point, the boys came up to visit me in Rhode Island, and I suggested we work on the Spanish course together, around the dining room table. The lessons were based on mimicry and spoken language, and Rocky would introduce a word, say it, and then ask you to repeat it before the little timer on the screen ran out. It was a way to test your fluency. There was a comprehension section where Rocky asked a question, and you had to respond in Spanish. It started off simple but became more challenging with each lesson.

We spent an afternoon on this together, and I observed both the differences in my son's learning styles and their different gifts when it came to language. Most of all, I saw how perfect they already were and how capable they were of learning the Spanish they wanted to learn.

Returning to El Yunque Rainforest in Puerto Rico for the first time since 1999 with my family. Not only did we have a great time, but I was unburdened of any shame about my Spanish fluency.

In fact, as I'm finishing this book, my family is enjoying another full-circle moment, this time in Puerto Rico. Roman has always wanted to visit *La Isla del Encanto*. The boys had the chance to visit the Dominican Republic with their mom a few years ago, but a trip to PR was still on the list. With Roman's 21st birthday this year, Noni and I decided this milestone moment was the right time to make it happen, and we surprised him with the news that we'd be going to Borínquen to celebrate his special day. Other than for quick layovers, I hadn't been to Puerto Rico since the late 90s, so this was meaningful for me as well.

I have loved the way we've woven Spanish, Spanglish, culture, history, food, music, and more on this trip. We're practicing our Spanish on car rides, in restaurants, and simply enjoying the spirit and hospitality of our Puerto Rican brothers and sisters. I'm feeling the freedom of not having to carry the weight of language shame, and ironically, my Spanish speaking is improving as a result. Because I'm simply not worried about it, I hope my family can sense that lightness in me as well.

In the end, what I keep learning, over and over, is that none of us grows while we are stuck in shame. Progress comes when we can begin to loosen our grip and step into a space that lets us play again. Dance taught me that, and that ability to feel connected, playful, and masterful in something that aligned with my identity was life-changing for me. Probably more life-changing than fluency in Spanish would have been, if I am being honest. It showed me that belonging can come from many directions and that feeling whole in one part of my identity can open doors in another.

So if you want to learn Spanish, go for it. And if you do not want to, that is fine too. What matters most is that you release the pressure long enough to rediscover lighthearted curiosity, because that is the only place where real learning can happen. My hope is that you take this conversation into your own life and your own communities. Be kind to each other, stand up for one another, and refuse any story that tells you or anyone else that you do not belong. Let this be the start of something, not the end.

ACKNOWLEDGEMENTS

"In their hearts humans plan their course, but the Lord establishes their steps."
—Proverbs 16:9

Lord knows I've tried to plan my own course many times and have not succeeded. Sometimes because I was just being shortsighted or immature. But I think mostly it's because God had something better planned for me. This book is one of those better things, and I want to first and foremost acknowledge God for His direction in my life. Even when I wasn't paying attention.

I always enjoy reading the acknowledgements page in a book because it's inspiring to see the depth of community it takes to get a work like this done. I never knew just how important that community was until writing my own.

I couldn't have asked for a better team than the one at Authors On Mission. I was supported with great care throughout the entire preparation, writing, and production phases of this process by a first-class team of professionals. Thank you, Dessa Broncate, for answering my thousand questions with velocity, patience, and a great sense of humor; Rachel Arterberry, for stewarding my manuscript over the finish line, painstakingly positioning all of my pictures during the holidays, and helping me set this book up for a successful launch. And thanks to the AOM team of designers, copy editors, content creators, and production professionals, whom I never met but who all helped make this book possible. Vikrant Shaurya, you've assembled a talented team and built a wonderful company that helps to get more essential stories out into the world.

Elise Fernbank, wow! You are the best thought partner, editor, and collaborator I could have ever had! Thank you for tenderly and thoughtfully walking with me as these memories and insights came to life and for demonstrating how much this story meant to you personally. Thank you for challenging me when necessary and encouraging me to lean in when I wanted to pull away. When this hits the shelves, I'm going to raise a cup of matcha in your honor!

Mary Desir, thank you for being the first to see the value in this topic and for inviting me to present on it to your colleagues at John Hancock. That engagement kicked off a series of presentations that resulted in this book.

Big thanks and shout outs to the following individuals and organizations for giving me the platforms and opportunities to share and develop the messages and themes of this book: Addie Diaz and the Addie-Tude Cultural Arts Center; my dear friends from the Rhode Island Foundation's Equity Leadership Initiative; Christopher Llópiz and Olaia O'Malley Gorbea of the Puerto Rican Professional Association of Rhode Island (PRPARI); Peter Chung and Young Voices RI; Rebecca Twitchell and the team at half full llc; Jenny Bautista-Ravreby and Blue Cross/Blue Shield of Rhode Island; the Association of Independent Schools of New England (AISNE); the New York State Association of Independent Schools (NYSAIS); the National Association of Independent Schools (NAIS) People of Color Conference; Jessica Parker-White and the Caribbean Museum Center for the Arts in St. Croix; Katie Zaytoun and the Virgin Islands Social Dance Collaborative (VISDC); the Bronx Library Center of the New York Public Library;

Gary Milgrom and Nunzia Manginelli with the NYC Association of Foreign Language Teachers (NYCAFLT); and all of the schools who welcomed me onto your campuses and into your communities. Your support and friendship mean the world to me.

Bobby Matos and John Santos, thank you for writing the truly amazing song that inspired this work. Michael McFadin at Ubiquity Records, you said you were in the studio when they recorded it. I'm envious! Thank you for your support and for allowing me to share this song in the book.

Dr. AnaMaria Correa and Ilhiana Rojas Saldana: At different times and in your own ways, you have reminded me that my work in dance is more than diversion and leisure. It is essential and life-giving. Thank you both for encouraging me to stand in my power as an artist and an educator and know that it's enough.

Adriana Borzellino, we've been in the foxhole together for years, and your friendship, support, and thought partnership are everything. I look forward to reading your book soon!

Eleanor López, thank you for introducing me to the world of Salsa dance. My life has been forever changed.

Teddy Kern and Elena Iannucci, you created one of the most unique and loving dance communities ever. The effects of the work and relationships that Dance Manhattan fostered continue to reverberate around the world. Thank you for taking a chance on a green Salsa dancer and allowing me to develop and experiment there. It's where I grew up.

Pierre Dulaine and the entire team (past and present) of Dancing Classrooms: Words can't really describe the impact of this program in the lives of children, families, schools, communities, and the teaching artists that deliver it. What Pierre created in one school in 1994 has blossomed to reach hundreds of thousands of children around the world and inspire not one, but three amazing films and a musical! It was an absolute joy to write this book during the 20th anniversary year of *Mad Hot Ballroom* and revisit this film's impact. (Shout out to Amy Sewell and Marilyn Agrelo!) It is one of the great privileges of my life to have been a part of this team and I'm grateful to every colleague I've worked with and to every school and student that welcomed me as a teaching artist. I received way more than I gave.

Addie Diaz-Siverio, the Addie-Tude Dance Company, was like a second family to me. Your choreography was dope, but more importantly, the love and camaraderie among us was genuine. I'm proud to call you sister and friend, and I look forward to working with you more in the future. Manny Siverio, you're a rock and an inspiration as an artist, a family man, and a Boricua.

Mariana Parma, you continue to dazzle us with your talent, creativity, and joy of life! I love dancing and creating with you, and we're way overdue for another collaboration!

Leticia Peguero, thank you for your genuine friendship and the work you do in the world. Whether in philanthropy, community-building, the arts, or just running a 5K on New Year's Eve, you're a rock star! Seeing your daily fitness achievements on my Apple Watch keeps me on my game!

I'm told this book is a social memoir. As such, while I wanted to share my personal stories, I wanted those stories to be surrounded by the work of experts and researchers in the fields of language, dance, and race and ethnic studies. A full list is in the References section, but there are a few that I'd like to single out here for their generosity:

- Dr. Elaine Ruiz-López: You are more than family. Your work in education and leadership is not just inspirational to me, but to an entire generation of scholar-activists, and to a future generation of scholars whose lives have been blessed through the creation of the International Leadership Charter High School in the Bronx. Your legacy is cemented. Thank you for your expertise and example as an author.

- Dr. Jennifer Leeman: I emailed and you immediately said: "Yes!" Yours was the first book I read on sociolinguistics in the Latino community and I was honored that you responded to my random request and spent so much time with me. Thank you for your research and insight.

- Verónica Guevara: Thank you for inviting me to work with your colleagues and students while you were at the King School in Connecticut. More importantly, thank you for telling me about your own experiences with Spanish, identity, parenting, and teaching. Your practice of learning through play is a core assertion of this book.

- Mark Hugo López: It was the Pew Research Center's 2023 report on language shame in the Latino community that validated the feelings I've had my whole life. To speak with the person who leads that research team and has such a depth of personal experience with this topic was a gift.

- Guesnerth Josué Perea: You responded enthusiastically to my random screening request on IG for *Faith in Blackness,* and I was so grateful! But to finally meet up with you in Brooklyn and hear both your personal story and professional insights on Afro-Latinidad was amazing! Thank you for your work in both the faith and academic communities and for pointing me in the direction of the work of Juan Flores, Miriam Jiménez-Román, and Nancy López.

- Sita Frederick: Your story is so inspiring and I'm tremendously thankful for your contribution to this book. Thank you (and Leti!) for welcoming me as a collaborator on *What Do You Dance On?* It's taken me over a decade to realize how important that production is to me. You were ahead of your time. Or maybe I'm just a little slow. :)

Jason Craige Harris, Pierre Dulaine, Samí Haimán-Marrero, Angélica Infante-Green, Tanya Katerí Hernandez: Thank you for agreeing to read early versions of the manuscript. I'm deeply grateful for your time and support.

Minahil Khan, thank you for helping me raise my branding game. Your work is awesome!

To every single person who shared their story with me: THANK YOU! Whether on Zoom, by phone, or in person, I deeply appreciate the time you spent with me, the vulnerability and honesty with which you spoke about your relationship to language and parenting, and your affirmation of the necessity of this book. Whether your story made it into the text or not, please know that I am grateful that you opened up a tender part of your lives with me.

To my awesome siblings, Tony, Janet, Yvonne, Leslie, Lisa, Robert, and Dennis: thank you for telling your truth and for being there for countless moments of joy in my life.

Jeff Smith and Patricia Romero, you were both there for me at a vulnerable time in my life, and I'm eternally grateful for your support and mentorship. And for insisting that I take Spanish in high school! Your willingness to take young people under your wing has positively impacted so many people.

Dad, I miss you. I wasn't around much for those final years, but I'm grateful that you were surrounded by love and family before you left us. (*Grácias, Lizzy y toda la familia.*) Even with your skepticism over my career choices, I never doubted your pride in me. The *tumbao* that you played with your hands lives on in my feet. I love you.

Mom, it hasn't always been easy, but I am so grateful for you and your life. I was truly delighted when you agreed to share your story with me for this project, and in those exchanges, I've come to know you even more. Thank you for teaching me those first steps. I love you.

Judy, thank you for being such a loving and dedicated mom. God blessed us with exceptional sons, and their character is infinitely more important than their fluency in Spanish. :) Your love for them is bottomless.

Rodney Jr. and Roman: I hit the Dad Lottery! I'm more than proud of the young men you've become. I marvel at your loving and generous natures and your desire to be men of faith. I have particularly appreciated the ways that you've grown to embrace your Latinidad. I'm privileged to be your Dad and I love you.

Noni, you wrote these words on the Dedication page of your doctoral dissertation in 2016:

"I want to dedicate this dissertation to my husband Rodney Eric López. I do not think I would have been able to make it to this point without you by my side. You are my partner, my love, and my best friend."

I can't begin to express what it means to me to be able to echo these words back to you ten years later. I am in awe of who you are as an educator and a leader and the remarkable ways that you have grown since you wrote those words. But I love you for who you are as a human being and as my wife. I'm grateful for our partnership and the ways that we support each other. This book doesn't happen without you and I thank you for your unwavering belief in me and in this project. Thank you for letting me take over our shared living spaces with my laptop and various devices and for introducing me to CookUnity so I could just focus on work. I love how we do life side by side. I love you more than you love electric Coke!

REFERENCES

Chapter One: Mira Quién Baila

You can watch the clip of the mentioned interviews and performance at the YouTube link below:

https://www.youtube.com/watch?v=g-fraTjOjIQ

Chapter Two: "So He Won't Understand"

Cummins, Jim. *Linguistic Interdependence and the Educational Development of Bilingual Children*, Review of Educational Research, 1979.

Jelly-Schapiro, Joshua. *Island People: The Caribbean and the World.* Knopf-Doubleday Publishing Group, 2016.

McMains, Juliet. *Spinning Mambo Into Salsa: Caribbean Dance in Global Commerce.* Oxford University Press, 2015.

Meléndez-Badillo, Jorell. *Puerto Rico: A National History.* Princeton University Press, 2025.

Ruiz-Lopez, Elaine. *The Fight for Equity in the Bronx: Changing Lives and Transforming Communities One Scholar at a Time.* Advantage Media Group, 2024.

Chapter Three: Never Enough

Allard, Elaine; Mortimer, Katherine; Gallo, Sarah; Link, Holly; Wortham, Stanton. *Immigrant Spanish as Liability or Asset? Generational Diversity in Language Ideologies at School*, University of Pennsylvania, Graduate School of Education, GSE Publications, 2014.

Fuller, Janet M. and Leeman, Jennifer. *Speaking Spanish in the U.S.: The Sociopolitics of Language* (2nd Edition), Multilingual Matters, 2020.

Garces-Conejos Blitvich, Pilar. *"You are shamed for speaking it or for not speaking it good enough": The paradoxical status of Spanish in the US Latino community*, The Routledge Handbook of Language in Conflict, 2019.

Ramos, Paola. *Defectors: The Rise of the Latino Right and What It Means for America*, Random House, 2025.

Chapter Four: Memories from the Island

Algarín, Miguel and Pinero, Miguel, editors. *Nuyorican Poetry: An Anthology of Puerto Rican Words and Feelings*, William Morow, 1975.

Aparicio, Frances. Listening to Salsa: Gender, Latin Popular Music, and Puerto Rican Cultures, University Press of New England, 1998.

Leeman, Jennifer. The Sociopolitics of Multilingualism in the United States: The Intertwining of Language, Race and Nation. In J. Darquennes, J. C. Salmons, & W. Vandenbussche (Eds.), *Handbooks of Linguistics and Communication Science* (Pp 670–687). De Gruyter. Handbooks of Linguistics and Communication Science, 2025.

Meléndez-Badillo, Jorell. *Puerto Rico: A National History*. Princeton University Press, 2025.

Perez, Rosie. *¡Yo Soy Boricua, pa' que tu lo sepas!* Documentary film. Independent Film Channel (IFC) Canada and Moxie Firecracker Films, 2006.

Chapter Five: Abuelo's House

Allard, Elaine; Mortimer, Katherine; Gallo, Sarah; Link, Holly; Wortham, Stanton. *Immigrant Spanish as Liability or Asset?*

Generational Diversity in Language Ideologies at School, University of Pennsylvania, Graduate School of Education, GSE Publications, 2014.

Brown, Monica. *Neither Here Nor There: Nuyorican Literature, Home, and the "American" National Symbolic*, Ohio State University, 1998.

Meléndez-Badillo, Jorell. *Puerto Rico: A National History.* Princeton University Press, 2025.

Velázquez, Isabel. *Household Perspectives on Minority Language Maintenance and Loss: Language in the Small Spaces*, Multilingual Matters, 2025.

Chapter Six: Je M'appelle Robert: Learning French in the Bronx

Fuller, Janet M. and Leeman, Jennifer. *Speaking Spanish in the U.S.: The Sociopolitics of Language* (2nd Edition), Multilingual Matters, 2020.

Leeman, Jennifer. *The sociopolitics of multilingualism in the United States: The intertwining of language, race and nation*, Handbooks of Linguistics and Communication Science, 2025.

Perlin, Ross. *Language City: The Fight to Preserve Endangered Mother Tongues in New York*, Atlantic Monthly Press, 2024.

Chapter Seven: From Je Parle Français to Yo Hablo Español

Anzaldúa, Gloria. *Borderlands / La Frontera: The New Mestiza*, Aunt Lute Books, 2012.

Gustines, George. "The Guilt of Not Being Bilingual," *The New York Times*, October 17, 2025.
https://www.nytimes.com/2025/10/17/us/comic-books-spanish-language.html

Perlin, Ross. *Language City: The Fight to Preserve Endangered Mother Tongues in New York*, Atlantic Monthly Press, 2024.

Chapter Eight: Rodney's Black: Searching for Meaning in the Tangled Web of Linguistic and Racial Identity

Bustamante, Luis-Noé; Gonzalez-Barrera, Ana; Edwards, Khadijah; Mora, Lauren; and López, Mark Hugo. *Majority of Latinos Say Skin Color Impacts Opportunity in America and Shapes Daily Life*, Pew Research Center Report, 2021.

Bustamante, Luis-Noé; Gonzalez-Barrera, Ana; Edwards, Khadijah; Mora, Lauren; and López, Mark Hugo. *Measuring the racial identity of Latinos*, Pew Research Center Report, 2021.

Flores, Juan and Román, Miriam Jiménez. *Triple-Consciousness? Approaches to Afro-Latino Culture in the United States*, Latin American and Caribbean Ethnic Studies, 2009.

Gonzalez-Barrera, Ana. *About 6 million U.S. adults identify as Afro-Latino*, Pew Research Center, 2022.

López, Nancy; Vargas, Edward; Juarez, Melina; Cacari-Stone, Lisa; and Bettez, Sonia. *What's Your "Street Race"? Leveraging Multidimensional Measures of Race and Intersectionality for Examining Physical and Mental Health Status among Latinxs*. Sociology of Race and Ethnicity, American Sociological Association, 2017.

Meléndez-Badillo, Jorell. *Puerto Rico: A National History*. Princeton University Press, 2025.

Ramos, Paola. *Defectors: The Rise of the Latino Right and What It Means for America*, Random House, 2025.

Román, Miriam Jiménez and Flores, Juan. *The Afro-Latin@ Reader: History and Culture in the United States*, Duke University Press, 2010.

Chapter Nine: Kitchen Salsa: Cooking Up Dance Steps with My Mom

Aparicio, Frances. *Listening to Salsa: Gender, Latin Popular Music, and Puerto Rican Cultures*, University Press of New England, 1998.

Concepción, Alma. *Dance in Puerto Rico: Embodied Meanings*, Archivo de Alma Concepción, C1700, Manuscripts Division, Department of Special Collections, Princeton University Library, 2002.

Jelly-Schapiro, Joshua. *Island People: The Caribbean and the World.* Knopf-Doubleday Publishing Group, 2016.

Leymarie, Isabelle. *Cuban Fire: The Story of Salsa and Latin Jazz.* Continuum International Publishing Group, 2002.

McMains, Juliet. *Spinning Mambo Into Salsa: Caribbean Dance in Global Commerce.* Oxford University Press, 2015.

Renta, Priscilla. "Salsa Dance: Latino/a History in Motion," *Centro Journal*, Vol. XVI, no. 2, The City University of New York, 2002.

Chapter Ten: Finding Dance - Or Did it Find Me?

Concepción, Alma. *Dance in Puerto Rico: Embodied Meanings*, Archivo de Alma Concepción, C1700, Manuscripts Division, Department of Special Collections, Princeton University Library, 2002.

McMains, Juliet. *Spinning Mambo Into Salsa: Caribbean Dance in Global Commerce.* Oxford University Press, 2015.

Chapter Eleven: Mad Hot Ballroom

Booth, Eric. *Making Change: Teaching Artists and Their Role in Shaping a Better World*. 2023.

Dulaine, Pierre. *Taking the Lead: Memoir of a Dancing Life*, Dancing Without Borders Press, 2016.

Magsamen, Susan and Ross, Ivy. *Your Brain on Art: How Art Transforms Us*, Random House, 2023.

Sewell, Amy. *The Mad Hot Adventures of an Unlikely Documentary Filmmaker*, Grand Central Publishing, 2007.

Williams, Caroline. *Move: How the New Science of Body Movement Can Set Your Mind Free*, Hanover Square Press, 2022.

Chapter Twelve: "I Understand Everything When I'm Dancing!"

Amirrezvani, Anita. "The More You Shake, The Better You Feel: Defying Culture." *Inc., with Mambo. ARTicles* 4 (1998): 126-37.

Aparicio, Frances. *Listening to Salsa: Gender, Latin Popular Music, and Puerto Rican Cultures*, University Press of New England, 1998.

Brown, Brené. *Atlas of the Heart: Mapping Meaningful Connection and the Language of Human Experience*, Random House, 2021.

Grant, Adam. *Hidden Potential: The Science of Achieving Greater Things*, Viking, 2023.

Magsamen, Susan and Ross, Ivy. *Your Brain on Art: How Art Transforms Us*, Random House, 2023.

Matos, Bobby and Santos, John. *I Don't Speak Spanish, but I Understand Everything When I'm Dancing!* Musical recording, Album: *Mambo Jazz*, Ubiquity Records, 2001.

Chapter Thirteen: What Do You Dance On?

Flores, Juan. *Salsa Rising: New York Latin Music of the Sixties Generation*, Oxford University Press, 2016.

McMains, Juliet. *Spinning Mambo Into Salsa: Caribbean Dance in Global Commerce.* Oxford University Press, 2015.

Renta, Priscilla. "Salsa Dance: Latino/a History in Motion," *Centro Journal*, Vol. XVI, no. 2, The City University of New York, 2002.

Chapter Fourteen: Raising the Next Generation

Fuller, Janet M. and Leeman, Jennifer. *Speaking Spanish in the U.S.: The Sociopolitics of Language* (2nd Edition), Multilingual Matters, 2020.

Perlin, Ross. *Language City: The Fight to Preserve Endangered Mother Tongues in New York*, Atlantic Monthly Press, 2024.

Velázquez, Isabel. *Household Perspectives on Minority Language Maintenance and Loss: Language in the Small Spaces*, Multilingual Matters, 2025.

Chapter Fifteen: Healing Through Fatherhood

Alford, Natasha S. *American Negra: A Memoir*, Harper, 2024.

Brown, Brené. *Atlas of the Heart: Mapping Meaningful Connection and the Language of Human Experience*, Random House, 2021.

Blitvich, Pilar G. *"You are shamed for speaking it or for not speaking it good enough": The paradoxical status of Spanish in the US Latino community."* In *The Routledge Handbook of Language in Conflict*, pp. 398-415. Routledge, 2019.

Velázquez, Isabel. *Household Perspectives on Minority Language Maintenance and Loss: Language in the Small Spaces*, Multilingual Matters, 2025.

Epilogue: Dining Room Spanish

Grant, Adam. *Hidden Potential: The Science of Achieving Greater Things*, Viking, 2023.

Magsamen, Susan and Ross, Ivy. *Your Brain on Art: How Art Transforms Us*, Random House, 2023.

Williams, Caroline. *Move: How the New Science of Body Movement Can Set Your Mind Free*, Hanover Square Press, 2022.

www.ingramcontent.com/pod-product-compliance
Lightning Source LLC
Chambersburg PA
CBHW032010150726
47990CB00005B/1907